# healthy one pan dinners

# healthy one pan dinners

100 easy recipes for your sheet pan, skillet, multicooker, and more

Dana Angelo White, MS, RD, ATC

ALPHA

**Publisher** Mike Sanders
**Senior Editor** Ann Barton
**Senior Designer** Rebecca Batchelor
**Photographer** Kelley Schuyler
**Food Stylist** Savannah Norris
**Proofreaders** Lisa Starnes, Monica Stone
**Indexer** Brad Herriman

First American Edition, 2020
Published in the United States by DK Publishing
6081 E. 82nd Street, Indianapolis, Indiana 46250

Copyright © 2020 by Dana White Nutrition, Inc.

20 21 22 23 24    10 9 8 7 6 5 4 3 2 1
001-317280-JUN2020

Published in the United States by Dorling Kindersley Limited

ISBN: 978-1-46549-266-1
Library of Congress Catalog Number: 2019950714

**Note:** This publication contains the opinions and ideas of its author(s). It is intended to provide helpful and informative material on the subject matter covered. It is sold with the understanding that the author(s) and publisher are not engaged in rendering professional services in the book. If the reader requires personal assistance or advice, a competent professional should be consulted. The author(s) and publisher specifically disclaim any responsibility for any liability, loss, or risk, personal or otherwise, which is incurred as a consequence, directly or indirectly, of the use and application of any of the contents of this book.

**Trademarks:** All terms mentioned in this book that are known to be or are suspected of being trademarks or service marks have been appropriately capitalized. Alpha Books, DK, and Penguin Random House LLC cannot attest to the accuracy of this information. Use of a term in this book should not be regarded as affecting the validity of any trademark or service mark.

DK books are available at special discounts when purchased in bulk for sales promotions, premiums, fund-raising, or educational use. For details, contact
SpecialSales@dk.com

Printed and bound in China
All images © Dorling Kindersley Limited
For further information see: www.dkimages.com

A WORLD OF IDEAS:
SEE ALL THERE IS TO KNOW

www.dk.com

# contents

## dutch oven 72

## baking dish 102

## multicooker + slow cooker 128

# introduction

Getting dinners on the table night after night is a recipe for stress in many households. On top of deciding what to make, come the tasks of planning, shopping, prepping, cooking, and—my least favorite—cleaning!

I created this book because I am in the trenches with you—the dinner struggle is real. Hectic schedules, hungry kids, and my dietitian-workaholic mom brain have driven my love for creating recipes that are delicious and healthy (my top two criteria, in that order). But there's more—these recipes are also easy to make, made with seasonal ingredients, and have minimal prep and clean up. It may seem like an impossible feat, but it is doable.

Using a few staple pieces of cooking equipment and minimally processed, whole-food ingredients, these recipes are designed to alleviate your stress, elevate the nutrition, and bring everyone around the table. Your family will be so grateful, they may insist on doing the dishes.

# the **healthy one pan** kitchen

One pan cooking is all about simplicity. You won't find recipes in this book that call for hard-to-find ingredients or unusual cooking equipment. These recipes rely on basic kitchen equipment and ingredients you can easily source at your local supermarket.

## 6 Key Cooking Vessels

The recipes in this book were developed using six vessels, all of which are versatile and hardworking additions to any kitchen. We'll look at the attributes of each on the coming pages.

1. Sheet pan
2. Cast-iron skillet
3. Dutch oven
4. Baking dish
5. Slow cooker
6. Multicooker

## 10 Must-Have Ingredients

These fresh foods provide the nutritional power behind many of the recipes in this book. They are filled with protein, healthy fats, energy-producing carbs, and cell-protecting antioxidants.

1. Boneless, skinless chicken thighs
2. Frozen shrimp
3. Salmon
4. Lean ground beef and turkey
5. Extra-firm tofu
6. Eggs
7. Sweet potatoes
8. Bell peppers
9. Leafy greens, such as kale and spinach
10. Seasonal vegetables (Whatever you like!)

## 20 Kitchen Staples

Keeping these pantry items on hand ensures you are always ready to create just about any healthy one pan meal.

1. Kosher salt
2. Olive oil
3. Canola oil
4. Honey
5. Smoked paprika
6. Turmeric
7. Ground cumin
8. Reduced-sodium soy sauce or gluten-free tamari
9. Panko bread crumbs
10. Canned crushed tomatoes
11. Jarred marinara sauce
12. Rolled oats
13. Long-grain brown rice
14. Rice wine vinegar
15. Canned beans
16. Quinoa
17. Flour (all-purpose and whole-wheat pastry flours)
18. Pasta (regular and whole grain)
19. Boxed chicken and/or vegetable stock
20. Nuts and nut butters

# sheet pan

Basic aluminum sheet pans are indispensible in the kitchen. The rimmed edge helps to ensure food doesn't fall into the oven, which is never a fun job to clean up. I recommend keeping two or three of these on hand for everything from trays of roasted vegetables to double batches of cookies.

### Benefits

Sheet pans are inexpensive and versatile. They can stand up to high heat in the oven and offer a large, flat surface area—perfect for caramelizing foods.

### Best Uses

Roasted vegetables; roasted meat, poultry, and fish; pizza; baked goods.

### Sizes

My must-have sheet pan size is a half sheet pan, which is 13 x 18 inches. You can also find full sheet pans, which are double in size but may not fit in all ovens. Smaller quarter sheet pans are 9 x 13 inches and can be useful when preparing smaller quantities of food.

### Accessories

Parchment paper is essential to prevent sticking. (Just don't use it under the broiler—it will burn.) I like to buy precut sheets of parchment that exactly fit a half sheet pan—the best quality ones are found at Williams Sonoma or King Arthur Flour. You'll also need a spatula or tongs for turning food and oven mitts for removing hot pans from the oven.

### Functions

Roasting, broiling, baking.

### Cleaning Tips

For the easiest cleanup, line sheet pans with a layer of aluminum foil and then a sheet of parchment paper. Otherwise, they typically only need a quick wash in warm, soapy water.

Recommended brands: Chicago Metallic, Nordic Ware

# **cast-iron** skillet

Cast-iron skillets are arguably the most versatile vessels for one pan meals. Cast iron can go from stove top to oven with ease and is virtually indestructible— just keep in mind that these babies are heavy!

### Benefits
Cast iron stands up to high-heat cooking, searing, frying, roasting, and baking. Cooking with cast iron even helps to safely impart iron into food, contributing to your intake of this important mineral.

### Best Uses
Roasted chicken, fried rice, fish tacos, seared meats.

### Sizes
While you can find these pans anywhere from 3 to 15 inches in diameter, the standard size for a skillet is 12 inches. I also have a 10-inch pan, which is handy for smaller-batch recipes.

### Accessories
Wooden or silicone utensils are recommended to prevent scratching. Keep a good oven mitt nearby as the handle gets hot.

### Functions
Searing, sautéing, frying, baking.

### Cleaning Tips
A well-seasoned pan needs little more than warm water and some mild dish soap on occasion. You can scour cast iron with kosher salt, but avoid scrubbing with anything too abrasive, and don't leave your pan soaking in water. After washing, dry immediately and wipe the inside with a little oil.

Recommended brand: Lodge

# dutch
# oven

Everyone should have at least one of these sturdy pots. Usually made from cast iron, they have a tight-fitting lid and great heat retention.

## Benefits
This is the ideal vessel to move from stove top to oven. I love that I can boil pasta, drain it, and then bake it all in the same pot—any baked ziti fans out there? You can also proof and bake an amazing loaf of bread in a Dutch oven!

## Best Uses
Soup, pasta dishes, stews, frying.

## Sizes
Dutch ovens are available in many sizes. Most of the recipes in this book were developed using a 7¼-quart pot, but a few were made in a smaller version—the 4½-quart pot. A good intermediate option is a 5½-quart model.

## Accessories
As with cast-iron skillets, use nonstick utensils with a Dutch oven, and use caution (and oven mitts) as the handles get hot.

## Functions
Stewing, braising, baking, sautéing; also great for boiling pasta.

## Cleaning Tips
Mild soap and water should do the trick. Many Dutch ovens have an enamel coating that is easy to clean but can scratch and wear away if scrubbed too hard. If the outside of the pot becomes stained after a lot of use, a mild abrasive cleaner like Bar Keepers Friend can help make it look like new.

Recommended brands: Le Creuset, Lodge

# **baking** dish

Shallow baking dishes are the original one-pan-meal cooking vessel. They're perfect for casseroles and other oven-baked recipes.

### Benefits

These dishes are deeper than rimmed sheet pans, which helps keep food moist and tender. You can find baking dishes made from many materials, but glass or ceramic is my preference. Some dishes come with covers, perfect for making meals ahead, storing leftovers, and packing up for a pot luck.

### Best Uses

Casseroles, baked pasta dishes, baked goods.

### Sizes

There is a ton of variety in shapes and sizes for baking dishes. A rectangular 9 x 13-inch pan and a square 9 x 9-inch pan are the best choices for one pan dinners and are the sizes used for this book.

### Accessories

You'll need a large serving spoon for dishing up big scoops of casseroles and oven mitts to protect hands.

### Functions

Baking, roasting.

### Cleaning Tips

Warm, soapy water is typically all you need to clean a baking dish—don't forget to get in the corners. Many brands are also dishwasher safe.

Recommended brands: Le Creuset (ceramic), Pyrex (glass).

# multicooker or electric pressure cooker

The old-school pressure cooker has been reinvented, and more and more kitchens now have the (much safer) electric version. As it turns out, you can do so much more than pressure cook with these updated models.

### Benefits

Long gone are the days of exploding soups on the stove top. Once folks work up the courage to take their multicooker out of the box, they are hooked. Multicookers live up to the "multi" name and can be used to make a wide variety of foods including cheesecake, applesauce, yogurt, rice, and hard-boiled eggs.

### Best Uses

Soup, risotto, pulled meats, steamed seafood

### Sizes

Units range from 3- to 8-quart capacities. The recipes in this book were developed using a 6-quart model.

### Accessories

An inner rack allows you to steam foods as well as to cook multiple dishes in 2 or 3 layers in one cooking session. A good pair of tongs comes in handy to get foods in and out of the inner pot. I also use a pair of small silicone mitts to handle the pressure release gauge and inner pot.

### Functions

Most models have a number of preset functions, but my most-used setting is the basic pressure cooking mode. The saute mode is also useful for sautéing and searing food prior to pressure cooking, as well as for reducing sauces afterward.

### Cleaning Tips

The inner pot cleans easily with soap and water and the all-important sealing ring can be soaked or run through the dishwasher to remove any lingering odors.

Recommended brands: Instant Pot, Ninja

# slow cooker

Like pressure cookers, slow cookers have come a long way. Newer models incorporate features like programmable settings and saute functions. You can't get any better for low temperature and set-it-and-forget-it cooking.

### Benefits

Although some may be tempted to ditch their slow cooker once they have a multicooker with a slow cook function, I still find that slow cooker recipes are superior in a stand-alone unit. Basic models are also more affordable than a multicooker.

### Best Uses

Soups, stews, pulled/stewed meats.

### Sizes

Slow cookers can be anywhere from 4 to 8 quarts in capacity. For most people, a 6- or 7-quart slow cooker will be the best choice.

### Accessories

It's helpful to have wooden spoons, tongs, a slotted spoon, and a good ladle for soups.

### Functions

Basic models have settings for warm, low, and high slow cooking. More robust models offer programmable functions and greater heat control. They may also steam, brown, and sauté. The sauté setting is often useful for searing and simmering before or after slow cooking.

### Cleaning Tips

Clean the lid and pot with warm, soapy water. On many models, the inner pot is dishwasher safe.

Recommended brands: Cuisinart, Crock-Pot

15

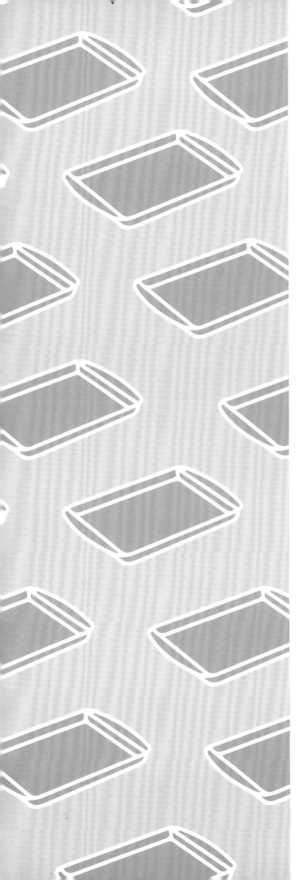

gluten-free **GF**
dairy-free **DF**
vegan **V**
under 30 minutes **30**
freezer friendly **FF**

# sheet pan

# **chicken** fajitas

Fajitas are always a popular weeknight dinner, and preparing them on a sheet pan is the simplest way to enjoy them. The flavorful chicken and vegetables can also be used to make delightful salads, rice bowls, and burritos.

Yield **6 servings** • Prep Time **15 minutes** • Cook Time **20 minutes** DF 30

1¾ lb boneless, skinless chicken breast

1 red onion, sliced

1 red bell pepper, sliced

1 green bell pepper, sliced

2 tbsp taco seasoning (see tip)

12 (6-in) flour tortillas, warmed

1 avocado, diced

¼ cup pickled jalapeños

Hot sauce, to serve

1. Preheat the oven to 425°F. Line a sheet pan with aluminum foil and parchment paper.

2. Cut the chicken into ½-inch strips and place in a resealable plastic bag along with the onion, peppers, and taco seasoning. Seal the bag and shake to coat the chicken and vegetables.

3. Spread the chicken and vegetables on the prepared sheet pan. Cook for 20 minutes or until chicken reaches an internal temperature of 160°F.

4. To serve, pile the chicken and vegetables on the flour tortillas and top with diced avocado, pickled jalapeños, and hot sauce.

5. Store leftovers in an airtight container in the refrigerator for up to 4 days.

**TIP** | To make your own taco seasoning, combine equal parts ground cumin, kosher salt, paprika, onion powder, garlic powder, and chili powder.

**VARIATION** | Make this recipe gluten-free by using corn tortillas or lettuce wraps instead of flour tortillas.

---

**NUTRITION PER SERVING (2 LOADED FAJITAS ON FLOUR TORTILLAS)**

Calories **369** • Total fat **12g** • Saturated Fat **2g** • Cholesterol **85mg** • Sodium **680mg** •
Total Carbohydrate **34g** • Dietary Fiber **3g** • Sugars **3g** • Protein **31g**

# lemon drumsticks with broccoli + sweet potatoes

Quick, easy, and healthy—this colorful dinner checks all the boxes. Chicken drumsticks get a zesty boost from lemon juice, and the broccoli and sweet potatoes are beautifully roasted. Try swapping in your favorite veggies!

Yield **4 servings**  •  Prep Time **10 minutes**  •  Cook Time **35 minutes**      GF   DF

8 chicken drumsticks

3 medium sweet potatoes, peeled and diced

1 tbsp olive oil

1 lemon, halved

½ tsp kosher salt

¼ tsp freshly ground black pepper

2 tsp dried seasoning blend (such as Greek or Italian seasoning)

2 cups broccoli florets

**1.** Preheat the oven to 450°F. Line a sheet pan with aluminum foil and parchment paper.

**2.** Arrange the drumsticks on one side of the sheet pan and the sweet potatoes on the other. Squeeze one lemon half over the chicken and sweet potatoes followed by a drizzle of olive oil. Sprinkle with salt, pepper, and seasoning blend, and lightly toss so both the chicken and sweet potatoes are evenly coated with seasoning.

**3.** Place in the oven and cook for 25 minutes. Remove the pan from the oven and add the broccoli on top of the sweet potatoes. Return to the oven and cook for an additional 10 minutes. Remove from the oven and squeeze the remaining lemon half over the top.

**NUTRITION PER SERVING**

Calories **558**  •  Total fat **28g**  •  Saturated Fat **7g**  •  Cholesterol **245mg**  •  Sodium **444mg**  •
Total Carbohydrate **23g**  •  Dietary Fiber **4g**  •  Sugars **5g**  •  Protein **51g**

# ginger shrimp with carrots + snap peas

Shrimp are a must-have protein source for speedy sheet pan meals. Make this is for a fast and easy weeknight dinner, or make a double portion for a week of meal-prepped lunches. Serve with cooked brown rice or noodles, if desired.

Yield **4 servings** • Prep Time **10 minutes** • Cook Time **12 minutes**

1 lb large shrimp, peeled and deveined

¾ lb sugar snap peas

3 large carrots, peeled and sliced

2 tbsp reduced-sodium soy sauce

1 tbsp sesame oil

1 tbsp honey

1 clove garlic, minced

2 tsp grated fresh ginger

Sesame seeds (optional), to garnish

Scallions, sliced, (optional), to garnish

Sriracha (optional), to serve

1. Preheat the oven to 400°F. Line a sheet pan with parchment paper.

2. Place the shrimp on one side of the sheet pan. Place the sugar snap peas in the middle of the pan and the carrots next to the peas.

3. In a small bowl, whisk together the soy sauce, sesame oil, honey, garlic, and ginger.

4. Pour the sauce over the shrimp and vegetables, tossing gently to coat. Place in the oven and roast for 10 to 12 minutes or until shrimp is pink and vegetables are slightly tender.

5. Remove from the oven and garnish with sesame seeds and chopped scallions. Serve with Sriracha, if desired.

**TIP** | Slice carrots on the bias or spiralize for fun texture and shape.

**VARIATION** | Swap asparagus for the snap peas when in season.

---

**NUTRITION PER SERVING (DOES NOT INCLUDE RICE OR NOODLES)**

Calories **185** • Total fat **4g** • Saturated Fat **0g** • Cholesterol **143mg** • Sodium **652mg** • Total Carbohydrate **20g** • Dietary Fiber **4g** • Sugars **4g** • Protein **21g**

# curry pork tenderloin with smashed potatoes + arugula

Pork tenderloin is filled with muscle-building protein and energy-boosting B vitamins. When roasted at high heat, it cooks quickly but remains tender and juicy. Golden, crispy potatoes and peppery arugula bring the meal together.

Yield **6 servings**  •  Prep Time **10 minutes**  •  Cook Time **35 minutes**

---

1 tbsp curry powder

1 tsp ground turmeric

1 tbsp light brown sugar

1 tsp smoked paprika

1 tsp kosher salt, divided

2 (1½lb) pork tenderloins

1 lb baby potatoes

2 tbsp olive oil

¼ tsp freshly ground black pepper

3 cups arugula

1. Preheat the oven to 450°F. Line a sheet pan with aluminum foil and parchment paper.

2. In a small bowl, combine the curry powder, turmeric, brown sugar, paprika, and ½ teaspoon salt.

3. Place the pork on one side of the sheet pan and rub with spice mixture. Arrange the potatoes next to pork and season with olive oil, remaining ½ teaspoon salt, and pepper. Transfer to the oven and cook for 20 minutes.

4. Remove the pan from the oven and using a sturdy spatula or mallet, gently press each potato to flatten. Return the pan to the oven and continue to cook until potatoes are tender and golden and pork has reached an internal temperature of 145°F.

5. Remove from the oven, and top the potatoes with the arugula, gently tossing to wilt the arugula. Slice the pork and serve with potatoes and arugula.

**TIP** | Use small, equal-sized potatoes to ensure even cooking.

---

**NUTRITION PER SERVING**

Calories **486**  •  Total fat **13g**  •  Saturated Fat **3g**  •  Cholesterol **166mg**  •  Sodium **528mg**  •  Total Carbohydrate **28g**  •  Dietary Fiber **4g**  •  Sugars **3g**  •  Protein **63g**

# potato skins for dinner

These 'tater skins aren't just bar food. To make this dinner in a weeknight jiffy, bake the potatoes ahead of time and store in the fridge until ready to use. Use whatever you have on hand for toppings, but be sure to include some high-protein ingredients to make for a satisfying meal.

Yield **4 servings** • Prep Time **15 minutes** • Cook Time **65–70 minutes**

4 medium russet potatoes

1 tsp olive oil

½ tsp kosher salt

1 cup canned black beans, drained and rinsed

½ cup salsa

1 cup shredded cheddar cheese

Plain nonfat Greek yogurt (optional), to serve

Fresh chives, chopped (optional), to serve

1. Preheat the oven to 425°F. Using a fork, poke a few holes in the potatoes and transfer to a sheet pan.

2. Place in the oven and bake until tender, 50 to 55 minutes. Allow to cool slightly.

3. When potatoes are cool enough to handle, slice lengthwise and use a spoon to scoop out the flesh. (Save the flesh for another use, such as mashed potatoes.)

4. Line a sheet pan with parchment paper. Place the potato skins on the pan, brush the inside of each skin with olive oil, and sprinkle with salt.

5. Fill each potato skin with black beans, followed by the salsa and cheese.

6. Bake for 15 minutes or until the cheese is melted and bubbly. Serve with Greek yogurt and chives, if desired.

**VARIATION** | Load up your potato skins with any toppings you desire! Other options include roasted vegetables and part-skim mozzarella; cooked chicken, barbecue sauce, diced tomato, and pepper jack cheese; or broccoli, cooked bacon, and cheddar.

**NUTRITION PER SERVING (2 PIECES)**

Calories **465** • Total fat **14g** • Saturated Fat **6.5g** • Cholesterol **30mg** • Sodium **667mg** •

Total Carbohydrate **66g** • Dietary Fiber **13g** • Sugars **4g** • Protein **22g**

# sheet pan **barbecue**

Take the barbecue inside with this sheet pan dinner. The ribs, corn, and beans are cooked together in the oven with very little hands-on time. Serve with coleslaw or greens for a complete meal.

Yield **6 servings**  •  Prep Time **20 minutes**  •  Cook Time **2 hours**  GF DF

---

2¾ lb St. Louis-style pork ribs

2 tsp smoked paprika

1 tsp ground fennel seed

2 tsp kosher salt

¼ cup barbecue sauce

**For the beans**

2 (15oz) cans pinto beans, drained and rinsed

3 tbsp molasses

2 tbsp ketchup

3 tbsp finely chopped onion

½ tsp garlic powder

Scallions, chopped, to garnish

**For the corn**

3 ears corn

3 tsp olive oil

Kosher salt

Freshly ground black pepper

**1.** Preheat the oven to 325°F. Trim any excess fat and membrane from the ribs and place on 2 large pieces of aluminum foil.

**2.** In a small bowl, mix the paprika, fennel seed, and salt. Rub the spice blend on both sides of the ribs. Wrap the ribs tightly in foil and place on a sheet pan.

**3.** In a small oven-safe dish, combine the beans, molasses, ketchup, onion, garlic powder and ⅓ cup water. Stir, cover loosely with foil, and place on the sheet pan next to ribs. Place in the oven and bake for 60 minutes.

**4.** Season the corn with olive oil, salt, and pepper, and wrap each piece in foil. After the ribs and beans have cooked for 60 minutes, remove the beans from the oven, and add the corn to the sheet pan.

**5.** Return the sheet pan to the oven. Cook for 30 minutes and then increase the heat to 375°F, unwrap ribs, baste with barbecue sauce, and cook for a final 30 minutes.

**6.** Before serving, warm beans in the microwave, if desired, and garnish with chopped scallions.

---

**NUTRITION PER SERVING**

Calories **598**  •  Total fat **15g**  •  Saturated Fat **4g**  •  Cholesterol **140mg**  •  Sodium **739mg**  •

Total Carbohydrate **61g**  •  Dietary Fiber **8g**  •  Sugars **18g**  •  Protein **50g**

# spatchcock herbed chicken
## with parsnips

It may sound ridiculous, but this method of cooking a whole chicken is the secret to perfectly cooked poultry with the most delicious crispy skin. Toss a few root veggies on the tray and let the amazing aroma permeate the kitchen.

Serves **6 servings**  •  Prep Time **15 minutes**  •  Cook Time **55 minutes**

1 (4–5lb) whole chicken

3 sprigs fresh rosemary

1 small bunch fresh thyme

1 lemon, sliced

2 lb parsnips, peeled and sliced

2 tbsp olive oil

2 tsp kosher salt

½ tsp freshly ground black pepper

1. Preheat the oven to 425°F. Line a sheet pan with aluminum foil and parchment paper. Place the rosemary, thyme, and lemon on the sheet pan.

2. Turn chicken over so it is breast-side down. Using a sharp knife or poultry shears, cut out the back bone and discard or reserve for stock.

3. Place the chicken on top of the herbs and lemon, breast-side up. Press down firmly on the center of the breast to flatten. (You will feel a pop.)

4. Scatter parsnips around the chicken, and drizzle everything with olive oil. Season with salt and pepper.

5. Transfer to the oven and cook for 45 to 55 minutes or until internal temperature of chicken reaches 160°F.

6. Allow to rest for 10 minutes before cutting chicken and serving with parsnips.

**VARIATION**  |  Replace parsnips with other root vegetables, such as carrots, celery root, or potatoes.

**NUTRITION PER SERVING**

Calories **501**  •  Total fat **19g**  •  Saturated Fat **4g**  •  Cholesterol **120mg**  •  Sodium **405mg**  •  Total Carbohydrate **27g**  •  Dietary Fiber **7.5g**  •  Sugars **7g**  •  Protein **45g**

# **meatball** heroes

I grew up calling these "subs" but my husband knows them as "heroes." In this case, it works. Meatballs tucked into warm rolls and smothered with sauce and cheese for fewer than 500 calories per serving? That's superhero-level delicious!

Yield **4 sandwiches** • Prep Time **30 minutes** • Cook Time **30 minutes**

1 lb 90% lean ground beef

1 large egg, beaten

3 tbsp panko bread crumbs

1 tbsp prepared pesto (see tip)

1 tsp kosher salt

½ tsp freshly ground black pepper

4 whole-grain sub rolls or hot dog rolls

¾ cup marinara sauce

¾ cup shredded part-skim mozzarella

**1.** Preheat the oven to 400°F. Line a sheet pan with parchment paper. Using a piece of aluminum foil, create a divider in the middle of the pan; this will prevent the juices from the meatballs from running all over the pan.

**2.** In a large bowl, combine the ground beef, egg, bread crumbs, pesto, salt, and pepper. With clean hands, gently mix well and form into 12 balls. Place the meatballs on one side of the prepared sheet pan. Bake for 20 minutes.

**3.** Remove from the oven and place 3 meatballs into each roll. Top each with sauce and cheese and return to the clean side of the sheet pan. Bake for 5 to 10 minutes, until the cheese is melted.

**4.** Serve warm, or let cool to room temperature, wrap in aluminum foil, and refrigerate or freeze.

**TIP** | Don't have pesto handy? Replace it with 1 tablespoon olive oil mixed with 1 teaspoon dried Italian seasoning.

**NUTRITION PER SANDWICH**

Calories **482** • Total fat **21g** • Saturated Fat **8g** • Cholesterol **131mg** • Sodium **831mg** •

Total Carbohydrate **40g** • Dietary Fiber **6g** • Sugars **8g** • Protein **34g**

# kale salad with roasted beets + crunchy chickpeas

Salads and sheet pans may not seem like a good matchup, but nothing makes a salad more exciting than roasted veggies and crunchy toppings. The highlight of this recipe is a protein boost from the addictive roasted chickpeas.

Yield **4 servings** • Prep Time **10 minutes** • Cook Time **45 minutes**

½ lb (4 medium) beets, peeled and cut into ¾-in pieces

1 (15oz) can chickpeas, drained and rinsed

2 tbsp olive oil, plus more to taste

1 tsp kosher salt, plus more to taste

Freshly ground black pepper, to taste

⅓ cup sliced almonds

8 cups chopped kale

Juice of 1 lemon

¼ cup chopped fresh chives

1 orange, peeled and segmented

½ cup crumbled feta cheese

**1.** Preheat the oven to 375°F. Line a sheet pan with parchment paper.

**2.** Place the beets on the left side of the sheet pan. Pat chickpeas dry with a clean kitchen towel and place on the right side of the sheet plan, leaving a few inches of space between the beets and the chickpeas.

**3.** Drizzle the beets and chickpeas with 2 tablespoons olive oil and season with salt and pepper to taste. Transfer to the oven and bake for 40 minutes, turning the pan once.

**4.** After 40 minutes, add the sliced almonds to the open center portion of the sheet pan and bake for an additional 5 minutes or until nuts are toasted and slightly golden.

**5.** Place the kale in a large bowl and toss with the lemon juice, using your hands to massage it into the leaves. Add the roasted beets, chickpeas, and almonds. Toss well, drizzle with another 2 to 3 teaspoons of olive oil, and season with additional salt and pepper, if desired. Top with the chives, orange segments, and feta.

**6.** Store leftovers in an airtight container in the refrigerator for 1 to 2 days.

**TIP** | For perfectly chopped kale, place roughly cut pieces (stems removed) in a bowl and cut into small pieces using sharp kitchen shears.

**VARIATION** | If you prefer romaine lettuce or baby spinach, follow the same method but make sure beets and chickpeas are fully cooled before tossing.

**NUTRITION PER SERVING**

Calories **406** • Total fat **23g** • Saturated Fat **5g** • Cholesterol **17mg** • Sodium **594mg** • Total Carbohydrate **41g** • Dietary Fiber **11g** • Sugars **11g** • Protein **16g**

# teriyaki shrimp stir-fry

A new one pan version of stir-fry is always a fabulous way to get your kids to eat more seafood. Keep frozen shrimp on hand and run under water to thaw just before cooking. Serve with brown rice or noodles for a complete meal.

Yield **4 servings** • Prep Time **10 minutes** • Cook Time **15 minutes**　　　DF　 30

2 tbsp reduced-sodium soy sauce

1 tbsp honey

2 tsp cornstarch

2 tsp grated fresh ginger

1 clove garlic, minced

1 lb large shrimp, peeled and deveined

6 cups broccoli florets

1 red onion, chopped

1 red bell pepper, chopped

Sesame seeds, to garnish

4 cups cooked brown rice, to serve

**1.** Preheat the oven to 425°F. Line a sheet pan with aluminum foil and parchment paper.

**2.** In a small bowl, combine the soy sauce, honey, cornstarch, ginger, and garlic; whisk well.

**3.** Place the shrimp and vegetables on the prepared sheet pan. Drizzle with the sauce and toss to coat.

**4.** Place in the oven and cook for 15 minutes, turning 1 to 2 times during cooking. Remove from the oven and sprinkle with sesame seeds. Serve over rice.

**5.** Store leftovers in an airtight container for up to 4 days.

---

**NUTRITION PER SERVING (INCLUDES 1 CUP OF COOKED RICE)**

Calories **470** • Total fat **5g** • Saturated Fat **1g** • Cholesterol **278mg** • Sodium **579mg** • Total Carbohydrate **60g** • Dietary Fiber **8g** • Sugars **10g** • Protein **40g**

# **popcorn chicken** dinner

Who needs frozen nuggets when you can make a tastier and healthier from-scratch version from start to finish in less than an hour? Coat the chicken ahead of time and keep in the fridge until ready to bake.

Yield **4 servings** • Prep Time **15 minutes** • Cook Time **20 minutes**     DF

2 cups all-purpose flour

2 eggs, beaten

3 cups cornflake crumbs (see tip)

1½ tsp kosher salt, divided

4 boneless, skinless chicken breasts, each cut into 8 pieces

2 medium zucchini, sliced

2 cups whole mushrooms, halved

2 tbsp olive oil

¼ tsp freshly ground black pepper

1 tbsp balsamic vinegar

**1.** Preheat the oven to 400°F. Line a sheet pan with aluminum foil and parchment paper.

**2.** Set up a breading station with the flour, beaten eggs, and cornflake crumbs each in a separate shallow bowl. Season each bowl with ¼ teaspoon salt.

**3.** Working in batches, dredge the chicken first in flour, then in egg, and then in the cornflake crumbs.

**4.** Place the breaded chicken pieces on one side of the sheet pan. Add the zucchini and mushrooms to the other side of the pan. Drizzle the vegetables with olive oil, remaining ¾ teaspoon salt, pepper, and vinegar.

**5.** Bake for 20 to 25 minutes until vegetables are tender and chicken is cooked through.

**TIP** | Look for boxes of premade cornflake crumbs in the baking aisle of the grocery store, or crush cornflake cereal in a food processor.

**NUTRITION PER SERVING**

Calories **420** • Total fat **12g** • Saturated Fat **2g** • Cholesterol **119mg** • Sodium **471mg** •

Total Carbohydrate **48g** • Dietary Fiber **3g** • Sugars **7g** • Protein **32g**

# healthy dinner **nachos**

Nachos for dinner? Absolutely! You can enjoy this famously high-calorie food in a more sensible fashion. Whole-grain chips are piled high with ingredients that boost the protein, fiber, and antioxidants in this vegetarian recipe.

Yield **6 servings**  •  Prep Time **10 minutes**  •  Cook Time **10 minutes**

1 (10oz) bag whole-grain tortilla chips

1 (15oz) can black beans, drained and rinsed

½ red onion, chopped

1 small zucchini, thinly sliced

1 cup shredded cheddar cheese

1 cup cherry tomatoes, halved

1 cup radishes, thinly sliced

1 cup grated carrots

1 avocado, diced

½ cup fresh cilantro leaves

6 oz plain low-fat Greek yogurt

Lime wedges, to serve

**1.** Preheat the oven to 400°F. Spread the tortilla chips on a sheet pan in an even layer.

**2.** Top the chips with black beans, red onion, and zucchini, and sprinkle with cheese. Bake for 8 to 10 minutes or until cheese is melted.

**3.** Remove from the oven and top with cherry tomatoes, radishes, carrot, avocado, cilantro and dollops of Greek yogurt. Serve warm with lime wedges.

**TIP** | Line the sheet pan with a layer of aluminum foil followed by a layer of parchment paper for easy clean up.

**VARIATION** | This recipe is endlessly adaptable. Mix it up with your favorite cheese, beans, and seasonal vegetables—or for an extra kick, sprinkle with chili powder before baking.

**NUTRITION PER SERVING**

Calories **433**  •  Total fat **23g**  •  Saturated Fat **6g**  •  Cholesterol **20mg**  •  Sodium **393mg**  •

Total Carbohydrate **45g**  •  Dietary Fiber **8g**  •  Sugars **7g**  •  Protein **14g**

# sheet pan **pancakes**

Who doesn't love breakfast for dinner? Instead of scurrying to flip pancakes as fast as they are eaten, make pancakes for a crowd with a sheet pan. Serve with scrambled eggs and fresh fruit for a complete meal.

Yield **8 servings**  •  Prep Time **10 minutes**  •  Cook Time **25 minutes**

½ cup whole-wheat pastry flour

1 cup all-purpose flour

½ tsp baking powder

½ tsp baking soda

1 tsp kosher salt

2 tbsp sugar

2 cups low-fat buttermilk

2 eggs, lightly beaten

3 tbsp unsalted butter, melted

Pure maple syrup (optional), to serve

Seasonal fruit (optional), to serve

1. Preheat the oven to 350°F. Spray a sheet pan with nonstick cooking spray.

2. In a large bowl, combine the whole-wheat flour, all-purpose flour, baking powder, baking soda, salt, sugar, buttermilk, eggs, and melted butter. Mix until just combined and pour the batter into the prepared pan.

3. Bake for 20 to 25 minutes or until puffed and cooked through. Cut into squares and serve topped with maple syrup and fruit, if desired.

4. Leftovers freeze beautifully; just wrap in parchment and place in a resealable plastic bag.

**VARIATION**  |  Can be made gluten-free by using a gluten-free pancake mix or swapping the flours for gluten-free baking mix.

---

**NUTRITION PER PANCAKE (NO FRUIT OR SYRUP)**

Calories **176**  •  Total fat **7g**  •  Saturated Fat **4g**  •  Cholesterol **63mg**  •  Sodium **356mg**  •  Total Carbohydrate **20g**  •  Dietary Fiber **2g**  •  Sugars **6g**  •  Protein **6g**

# **egg** sandwiches

These sandwiches are a breakfast-for-dinner favorite that can easily be customized with your favorite veggies and cheeses. Get creative and play with whatever you already have in the fridge or pantry.

Yield **6 servings**  •  Prep Time **7 minutes**  •  Cook Time **13 minutes**       30  FF

6 large eggs

¼ tsp kosher salt

2 tbsp low-fat milk

½ red bell pepper, diced

½ cup chopped broccoli

3 tbsp chopped chives

6 slices cheese (pepper jack recommended)

6 toasted rolls or English muffins

**1.** Preheat the oven to 400°F. Line a quarter sheet pan (9 x 13 inches) with parchment paper and spray with nonstick cooking spray.

**2.** In a medium bowl, whisk the eggs until well beaten. Add the salt, milk, bell pepper, broccoli, and chives, and mix to combine.

**3.** Pour the egg mixture into the prepared sheet pan and carefully place in the oven. Bake for 10 minutes.

**4.** Remove the pan from the oven and top with slices of cheese. Return to the oven for 2 to 3 minutes more to melt the cheese.

**5.** When ready to serve, use a knife or pizza cutter to cut the cooked eggs and cheese into 6 servings. Use a spatula to remove from the pan.

**6.** Serve on toasted rolls or English muffins. Sandwiches can be individually wrapped and frozen for up to 3 months.

**VARIATION**  | Add your favorite toppings, such as ham or avocado.
Make gluten-free with gluten-free rolls or gluten-free bread.
For a dairy-free version, add your favorite nut milk to the egg mixture and omit the cheese.

**NUTRITION PER SERVING**

Calories **314**  •  Total fat **16g**  •  Saturated Fat **7g**  •  Cholesterol **246mg**  •  Sodium **465mg**  •

Total Carbohydrate **24g**  •  Dietary Fiber **3g**  •  Sugars **2g**  •  Protein **20g**

# **cod** en papillote

This French method of steaming fresh vegetables and fish in parchment results in tender, flaky fish permeated with the aromatic flavors of lemon and thyme. It's a simple technique that looks sophisticated but is easy to achieve. The only thing better than this quick, high-protein recipe is the minimal cleanup.

Yield **4 servings** • Prep Time **15 minutes** • Cook Time **20 minutes**  GF  30

2 cups peeled and julienned sweet potato

1 cup thinly sliced red onion

1 cup thinly sliced bell pepper

1 lb cod, cut into 4 pieces

4 tbsp unsalted butter

8 sprigs fresh thyme

4 slices lemon

1 tsp kosher salt

**1.** Preheat the oven to 425°F. Prepare 4 sheets of parchment paper (12 x 16 inches each). Fold each in half and then unfold.

**2.** Place a pile of sweet potato strips, onion, and bell pepper on one side of each piece of parchment and top with a piece of cod. Top each piece of fish with 1 tablespoon butter, 2 sprigs thyme, and a slice of lemon; season with salt.

**3.** Fold the parchment over the fish. Starting at one end, fold the edges over, making overlapping pleats to seal the parchment around the fish, creating a half-moon-shaped packet. Be sure the edges are folded tightly so that the steam cannot escape. Repeat to fold the remaining packets.

**4.** Transfer the packets to a sheet pan. Bake for 20 minutes. Remove from the oven and allow to cool for 5 minutes before opening.

---

**NUTRITION PER SERVING**

Calories **297** • Total fat **12g** • Saturated Fat **7g** • Cholesterol **79mg** • Sodium **380mg** • Total Carbohydrate **14g** • Dietary Fiber **2g** • Sugars **3g** • Protein **21g**

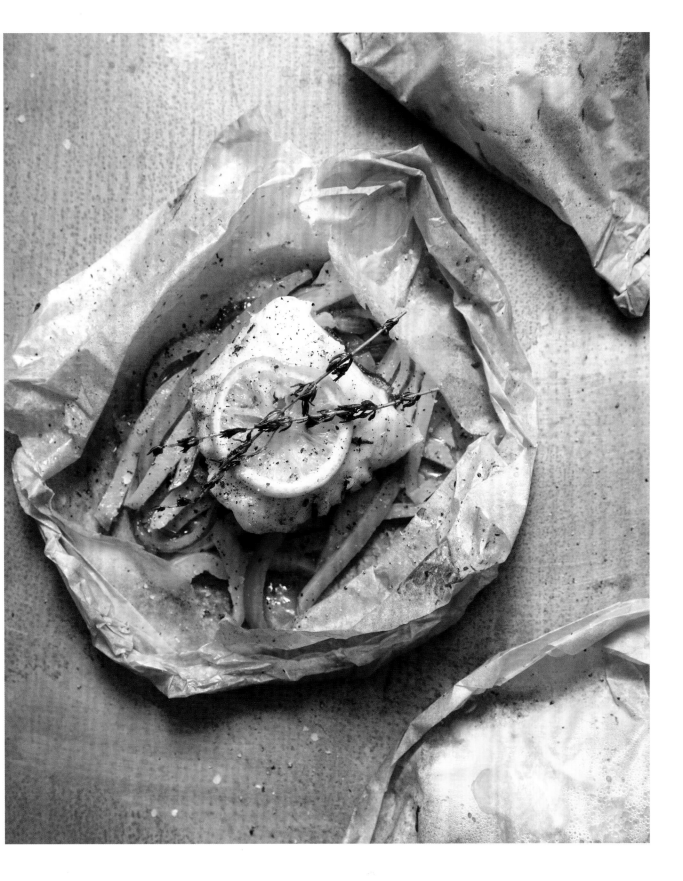

# roasted chicken thighs
## with butternut squash

Sometimes the simplest recipes are the best—two main ingredients, a sprinkle of seasoning, and a quick trip to the oven. Pile this incredible, flavorful chicken and squash on a salad or over a fluffy bed of rice or couscous.

Yield **4 servings**  •  Prep Time **10 minutes**  •  Cook Time **40 minutes**

1¾ lb boneless, skinless chicken thighs

6 cups chopped butternut squash

1 tbsp olive oil

1 tsp kosher salt

½ tsp red pepper flakes

1 tbsp dried Italian seasoning

**1.** Preheat the oven to 425°F. Line a sheet pan with aluminum foil and parchment paper.

**2.** Place the chicken thighs on the sheet pan and surround them with the chopped butternut squash. Season with olive oil, salt, red pepper flakes and Italian seasoning.

**3.** Bake for 35 to 40 minutes or until squash is tender and chicken reaches an internal temperature of 165°F.

**4.** Store leftovers in an airtight container in the refrigerator for 3 to 4 days.

**TIP** | Need to get more iron? Chicken thighs are an excellent source.

**NUTRITION PER SERVING**

Calories **310**  •  Total fat **11g**  •  Saturated Fat **2g**  •  Cholesterol **173mg**  •  Sodium **490mg**  •  Total Carbohydrate **14g**  •  Dietary Fiber **2g**  •  Sugars **6g**  •  Protein **40g**

# miso-glazed salmon
## with roasted bok choy

Preparing fish can be intimidating, but there's nothing to fear with this simple recipe. There's no better way to get omega-3 fats than a serving of salmon. These healthy fats benefit your skin, heart, eyes, and brain.

Yield **4 servings**  •  Prep Time **5 minutes**  •  Cook Time **15 minutes**   DF  30

4 (8oz) pieces salmon

1 bunch bok choy, chopped (about 6 cups)

1 tbsp reduced-sodium soy sauce

Freshly ground black pepper, to taste

2 tbsp honey

2 tbsp white miso

1 clove garlic, minced

**1.** Preheat the oven to 425°F. Line a sheet pan with parchment paper.

**2.** Place the salmon skin-side down on one side of the sheet pan and spread the bok choy on the other side of the pan. Drizzle the soy sauce over the bok choy and season with pepper; toss to coat.

**3.** To prepare the glaze, in a small bowl, mix the honey, miso, and garlic. Brush the salmon with the glaze.

**4.** Bake for 12 to 15 minutes or until salmon is cooked as desired and the bok choy is crisp-tender. Allow to cool for 5 minutes before serving.

**5.** Refrigerate leftovers in an airtight container for up to 4 days.

---

**NUTRITION PER SERVING**

Calories **401**  •  Total fat **13g**  •  Saturated Fat **3g**  •  Cholesterol **102mg**  •  Sodium **560mg**  •

Total Carbohydrate **16g**  •  Dietary Fiber **3g**  •  Sugars **11g**  •  Protein **52g**

# sheet pan **pizza night**

Every Friday is pizza night in my house. I keep batches of homemade dough in the freezer (just defrost the night before) and every week is a new pizza-making adventure. Make the dough and prep toppings ahead of time, or for a real shortcut, purchase unbaked dough from your local pizzeria.

Yield **12 pieces**  •  Prep Time **1 hour 15 minutes**  •  Cook Time **17 minutes**    FF

1 cup marinara sauce (see tip)

4 oz sliced provolone cheese

1½ cups shredded part-skim mozzarella

**For the dough (makes enough for 2 pizzas)**

1 packet dry active yeast

1 tsp honey or granulated sugar

6 cups all-purpose flour

1 tbsp kosher salt

2 tbsp olive oil

**Suggested toppings**

Onions

Peppers

Zucchini

Corn

Kale

Roasted broccoli

Chicken sausage

Roasted squash

Fresh basil

Mushrooms

**1.** To make the dough, combine 2 cups warm water with yeast and honey (or sugar), whisk gently, and set aside for 15 minutes to allow the yeast to activate.

**2.** Place the flour and salt in the bowl of a stand mixer fitted with a dough hook attachment. Turn on the mixer and combine the flour and salt.

**3.** With the machine running on low, add the yeast mixture and olive oil. Increase the speed to medium, and continue to mix until the dough comes together in a ball, about 3 minutes. Turn off the machine and place the dough in an oiled bowl. Cover with a clean kitchen towel and let rise for at least 1 hour.

**4.** Preheat the oven to 450°F. Using a paper towel, grease a sheet pan with a few teaspoons of olive oil. Once the dough has risen, turn out onto a lightly floured surface and divide the dough in half.

**5.** Roll out one half of the dough and transfer to the prepared sheet pan. (The remaining dough can be refrigerated or frozen for later use.) Press the dough to the edges of the pan until it stretches across the entire pan. Top the dough with sauce, followed by the provolone, mozzarella, and any desired toppings.

**6.** Bake for 15 to 17 minutes, turning the pan once halfway through baking. Remove from the oven and allow to cool for 5 minutes before cutting.

**7.** To store, wrap in parchment paper and place in a resealable bag. Refrigerate for up to 4 days or freeze for up to 3 months.

**TIP** | To make your own marinara sauce, sauté ½ cup chopped onion, 2 cloves garlic (minced), and ½ teaspoon ground fennel seed in 2 tablespoons olive oil. Add 1 (28oz) can crushed tomatoes, season with salt and pepper, and simmer for at least 20 minutes, stirring occasionally.

**VARIATION** | For a whole-wheat crust, replace half the flour with whole-wheat pastry flour.

---

**NUTRITION PER SLICE (DOES NOT INCLUDE TOPPINGS)**

Calories **182**  •  Total fat **16g**  •  Saturated Fat **3g**  •  Cholesterol **16mg**  •  Sodium **318mg**  •

Total Carbohydrate **24g**  •  Dietary Fiber **1g**  •  Sugars **2g**  •  Protein **8g**

# spinach-ricotta calzone

One of my favorite spins on pizza night is a veggie-and-cheese-stuffed calzone. The pizza dough comes together quickly, or you can purchase dough from your local pizzeria. Using part-skim cheeses helps to keep the calories and fat in check.

Yield **4 servings**  •  Prep Time **1 hour 15 minutes (if making dough)**  •  Cook Time **20 minutes**    V   30   FF

3 cups baby spinach

2 cloves garlic, finely chopped

½ tsp kosher salt, plus more to taste

¼ freshly ground black pepper

16 oz pizza dough (see Sheet Pan Pizza Night, page 41)

4 oz sliced provolone cheese

¾ cup part-skim ricotta cheese

¾ cup shredded part-skim mozzarella

2 tsp olive oil

Coarse sea salt, for sprinkling

**1.** Preheat the oven to 450°F. In a medium bowl, mix the baby spinach, garlic, salt, and pepper.

**2.** On a lightly floured surface, roll out the dough into a rectangle and then transfer the dough to a sheet pan. Place slices of provolone cheese longways in the middle of the dough and top with the spinach mixture, followed by dollops of ricotta cheese. Sprinkle with shredded mozzarella.

**3.** Fold in the shorter ends 2 to 3 inches toward the middle, covering the edges of the filling. Then, starting with the long side closest to you, fold the dough over the filling and roll the calzone closed; make sure the calzone is seam side down. Brush the top of the calzone with olive oil and sprinkle with coarse salt. Cut a few slits in the top to allow the steam to escape.

**4.** Bake for 16 to 18 minutes, or until puffed and golden brown, turning the pan once halfway through baking. Allow to cool for at least 10 minutes before slicing into 8 pieces. Once cooled, freeze whole or sliced in an airtight container for up to 3 months.

**NUTRITION PER SERVING**

Calories **543**  •  Total fat **17g**  •  Saturated Fat **10g**  •  Cholesterol **50mg**  •  Sodium **691mg**  •
Total Carbohydrate **72g**  •  Dietary Fiber **3g**  •  Sugars **4g**  •  Protein **26g**

# watermelon panzanella
# with fresh mint

A delightful marriage of textures and flavors, this recipe will surely become a summertime favorite. Between the watermelon, cucumber, and tomato, this dish is a perfect way to stay hydrated on a hot summer day.

Yield **4 servings** • Prep Time **5 minutes** • Cook Time **15 minutes**

4 thick slices day-old bread, cubed (preferably whole-grain)

3 tbsp olive oil, divided

½ tsp kosher salt, divided

Freshly ground black pepper, to taste

3 cups cubed watermelon

1 medium tomato, chopped

¼ red onion, thinly sliced

1 cup chopped cucumber

2 tbsp chopped fresh mint

¼ cup crumbled feta cheese

½ tsp lemon zest

Juice of ½ lemon

**1.** Preheat the oven to 350°F.

**2.** Spread the bread on a sheet pan, drizzle with 1 tablespoon olive oil, and season with ¼ teaspoon salt and a pinch of black pepper. Bake until toasted, about 15 minutes. Remove from oven and allow to cool to room temperature.

**3.** In a large bowl, combine the toasted bread, watermelon, tomato, onion, cucumber, mint, and feta.

**4.** Add the lemon zest, lemon juice, remaining 2 tablespoons olive oil, and season with the remaining ¼ teaspoon salt and black pepper to taste. Toss well and serve.

**NUTRITION PER SERVING**

Calories **239** • Total fat **13g** • Saturated Fat **3g** • Cholesterol **8mg** • Sodium **383mg** •

Total Carbohydrate **26g** • Dietary Fiber **5g** • Sugars **12g** • Protein **7g**

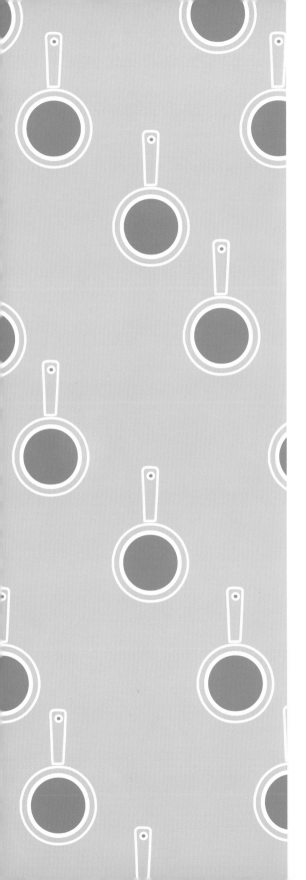

gluten-free GF
dairy-free DF
vegan V
under 30 minutes 30
freezer friendly FF

# skillet

# potato leek frittata

Frittatas spark joy! They are quick and easy, high in protein, filled with flavor, and look elegant, especially when made and served in a cast-iron skillet—the best pan for stove-to-oven cooking. This version features the classic combination of leeks and potatoes along with low-fat cheese.

Yield **4 servings**  •  Prep Time **10 minutes**  •  Cook Time **15 minutes**       GF  V  30  FF

1 tbsp olive oil

1 leek, white and light green parts only, thinly sliced

1 medium potato, thinly sliced

¾ tsp kosher salt

½ tsp freshly ground black pepper

8 eggs, beaten

1 cup part-skim shredded mozzarella

Fresh chives, chopped, to garnish

**1.** In a 10-inch cast iron skillet, heat the olive oil over medium-high heat. Add the leeks and potatoes and sauté until both are tender, about 5 minutes. Season with salt and pepper. Preheat the broiler to high.

**2.** Add the eggs to the pan and gently stir. Cook for 3 to 4 minutes more, until the eggs begin to set. Sprinkle with mozzarella and transfer to the broiler.

**3.** Broil for 2 to 3 minutes or until the cheese is melted and slightly golden. Remove from the broiler, sprinkle with chives, and serve warm or at room temperature.

**4.** Store leftovers in the refrigerator for up to 3 days or in the freezer for 1 month.

**TIP**  |  For perfect thinly sliced potatoes, use a handheld mandoline slicer.

**NUTRITION PER SERVING**

Calories **332**  •  Total Fat **17g**  •  Saturated Fat **6g**  •  Cholesterol **342mg**  •  Sodium **543mg**  •
Total Carbohydrate **24g**  •  Dietary Fiber **3g**  •  Sugars **2g**  •  Protein **22g**

# weeknight
# **chicken pot pie**

The ultimate comfort food, only easier and healthier. Many chicken pot pie recipes can tip the scales at more than 600 calories per serving, but with less butter and low-fat milk, this version is significantly lighter.

Yield **6 servings**  •  Prep Time **12 minutes**  •  Cook Time **35 minutes**              FF

1 tbsp olive oil

1 small onion, diced

2 medium carrots, diced

2 celery stalks, diced

2 tsp dried thyme

1 tsp kosher salt

½ tsp freshly ground black pepper

2 tbsp all-purpose flour

1 cup chicken stock

½ cup low-fat milk

3½ cups cooked, diced chicken

2 cups frozen mixed vegetables

1 (16oz) package unbaked biscuit dough (Trader Joe's suggested)

**1.** Preheat the oven to 375°F. In a 12-inch cast-iron skillet, heat the olive oil over medium-high heat. Add the onion, carrot, and celery, and sauté for 5 minutes.

**2.** Season with the thyme, salt, and pepper. Sprinkle with flour and cook for 2 to 3 minutes. Stir in the chicken stock and milk and simmer until thickened, about 2 minutes more. Stir in the chicken and vegetables and turn off heat.

**3.** Arrange the biscuits on top and transfer to the oven. Bake for 20 to 25 minutes or until top is golden brown. Serve warm.

**4.** To freeze, allow to cool completely and transfer to a freezer-safe container. Freeze for up to 3 months. To reheat, place in an oven-safe dish and place directly in the oven. Bake at 350°F for 40 to 45 minutes.

**TIP** | The filling can be made ahead and refrigerated for up to 2 days. When ready to serve, top with the biscuits and bake.

**NUTRITION PER SERVING**

Calories **402**  •  Total Fat **14g**  •  Saturated Fat **2.5g**  •  Cholesterol **64mg**  •  Sodium **852mg**  •

Total Carbohydrate **39g**  •  Dietary Fiber **5g**  •  Sugars **6g**  •  Protein **30g**

# pesto turkey meatballs
## with orzo

A satisfying meal in just one skillet! Herbaceous pesto boosts the flavor throughout the dish, and using lean ground turkey keeps it light yet filling.

Yield **4 servings** • Prep Time **10 minutes** • Cook Time **20 minutes**

---

1 lb 90% lean ground turkey

1 large egg, beaten

½ cup whole-wheat panko bread crumbs

3 tbsp prepared pesto, divided (see tip)

Kosher salt, to taste

Freshly ground black pepper, to taste

2 tsp olive oil

½ cup chopped onion

1 cup uncooked orzo pasta

2½ cups low-sodium chicken stock

3 cups broccoli florets

Parmesan cheese (optional), to serve

1. In a large bowl, combine the ground turkey, egg, bread crumbs, and 1 tablespoon pesto. Season with salt and pepper. With clean hands, gently mix well and form into 8 balls.

2. In a cast-iron skillet, heat the olive oil over medium-high heat. Add the meatballs and cook until browned on all sides, about 8 minutes. Transfer to a plate lined with paper towel.

3. To the same skillet, add the onion and remaining 2 tablespoons pesto and sauté for 1 minute. Add the orzo and toss to coat in the sauce, cooking for another 1 to 2 minutes to gently toast the orzo.

4. Stir in the chicken stock, increase the heat to high, and bring to a simmer. Add the meatballs back to the skillet along with broccoli florets. Reduce the heat to low, cover, and cook for 10 minutes or until orzo is tender and the meatballs are cooked through. Top with Parmesan cheese (if using) and serve.

5. Store in an airtight container in the refrigerator for 3 to 4 days, or freeze for up to 3 months.

**TIP** | Make your own pesto by combining 4 cups fresh basil, 2 cloves garlic, juice of 1 lemon, ¼ cup toasted pine nuts or walnuts (or omit nuts), salt, and pepper in a food processor. With the machine running, pour in about 1 cup olive oil, or until the sauce reaches desired consistency.

**NUTRITION PER SERVING**

Calories **483** • Total Fat **19g** • Saturated Fat **4g** • Cholesterol **130mg** • Sodium **311mg** • Total Carbohydrate **45g** • Dietary Fiber **4g** • Sugars **4g** • Protein **35g**

# hash brown quiche

This crave-worthy, gluten-free alternative to traditional quiche has a crust made from shredded potatoes. Broccoli, mushrooms, and bell pepper are a winning combination, but you can make the filling with any veggies you like. Cast iron goes from stove top to oven and cooks eggs evenly.

Yield **6 servings** • Prep Time **10 minutes** • Cook Time **25 minutes**

1 tbsp canola oil

3 cups shredded frozen hash browns

½ tsp kosher salt, divided

8 eggs

3 tbsp low-fat milk

½ tsp freshly ground black pepper

1 cup chopped broccoli

1 cup sliced mushrooms

1 bell pepper, any color, diced

1 cup shredded cheddar cheese

1. Preheat the oven to 400°F. In a cast-iron skillet, heat the canola oil over medium-high heat. Add the hash browns and sauté for 4 to 5 minutes. Season with ¼ teaspoon salt and spread the hash browns in an even layer at the bottom of the skillet. Remove from heat and set aside.

2. In a medium bowl, whisk the eggs and milk. Season with the remaining ¼ teaspoon salt and pepper.

3. Pour the eggs into the skillet, over the hash browns, and top with the broccoli, mushrooms, bell pepper, and cheese. Transfer to the oven and bake until the eggs are set, about 15 to 20 minutes. Remove from the oven and allow to cool slightly before slicing.

4. Cooled quiche can be stored in an airtight container in the refrigerator for 3 to 4 days and in the freezer for up to 1 month.

**TIP** | Freeze individual portions and reheat in the microwave for a superfast breakfast.

**VARIATION** | For a beautiful presentation, serve slices of quiche upside down so the crispy potatoes are on top.

**NUTRITION PER SERVING**

50  Calories **359** • Total Fat **14g** • Saturated Fat **6g** • Cholesterol **239mg** • Sodium **470mg** • Total Carbohydrate **41g** • Dietary Fiber **6g** • Sugars **2g** • Protein **16g**

# roasted chicken
## with root vegetables

A cast-iron skillet is the ideal cooking vessel for roasted chicken. Surround the chicken with flavorful root vegetables, and you have a complete, healthy meal ready in about an hour. Skip the skin, but enjoy both the breast and dark meat.

Yield **6 servings** • Prep Time **20 minutes** • Cook Time **60 minutes**   GF DF

1 (4lb) chicken

1 small bunch fresh thyme

3 sprigs fresh rosemary

½ lemon

3 cloves garlic

6 cups chopped mixed root vegetables, such as carrots, onion, sweet potato, Yukon gold potato

2 tbsp olive oil

2 tsp kosher salt

Freshly ground black pepper

**1.** Preheat the oven to 425°F. Place the chicken in the center of a 12-inch cast-iron skillet; pat the skin dry. Place the thyme, rosemary, lemon, and garlic in the cavity and tie the legs together using kitchen twine.

**2.** Spread root vegetables around the entire chicken and then drizzle chicken and vegetables with olive oil; season with salt and pepper to taste. Place in the oven for 60 minutes or until the chicken reaches an internal temperature of 165°F.

**3.** Carefully remove the skillet from the oven and allow to rest for 15 minutes before transferring the chicken to a cutting board to carve. Store leftovers in the refrigerator for up to 4 days.

**TIP** | Save the chicken carcass to make homemade stock. Place it in a large stock pot and cover with water; add onion, carrot, celery, kosher salt, peppercorns, bay leaf, and fresh herbs. Bring to a boil and reduce heat to low. Simmer for at least 3 hours or until the stock reaches your desired flavor.

**NUTRITION PER SERVING**

Calories **467** • Total Fat **20g** • Saturated Fat **4g** • Cholesterol **120mg** • Sodium **405mg** •

Total Carbohydrate **19g** • Dietary Fiber **3g** • Sugars **5g** • Protein **42g**

# shakshuka with kale

Simmer eggs in a delicious bath of tomatoes and vegetables. Using canned tomatoes increases the cell-protecting antioxidant power. Serve with warm pita bread or roasted potatoes.

Yield **4 servings**  •  Prep Time **10 minutes**  •  Cook Time **35 minutes**

1 tbsp olive oil

½ onion, sliced

1 bell pepper, sliced

2 cloves garlic, chopped

1 (28oz) can crushed tomatoes

4 cups chopped kale

½ tsp kosher salt

½ tsp ground cumin

4 eggs

⅓ cup crumbled feta cheese

½ cup chopped fresh parsley

**1.** Preheat the oven to 400°F. In a cast-iron skillet, heat the olive oil over medium-high heat. Add the onion and pepper and cook for 10 minutes, stirring occasionally.

**2.** Add the garlic, crushed tomatoes, kale, salt, and cumin. Stir well. Add 1 cup water and allow to simmer over medium heat for 15 minutes.

**3.** Using a large spoon, create a well in the tomato mixture and gently crack an egg into it. (To help ensure egg yolks don't break, crack the eggs into a small bowl before gently pouring into the skillet.) Repeat with the remaining eggs.

**4.** Transfer the skillet to the oven and cook for 8 to 10 minutes, or until eggs are cooked to desired doneness.

**5.** Remove from the oven and top with feta and parsley before serving. Store leftovers in an airtight container in the refrigerator for up to 4 days.

**TIP** | You can freeze the tomato mixture, reheat, and add the eggs when ready to serve.

**VARIATION** | To add more protein and texture, toss in 1½ cups canned chickpeas with the kale in step 2.

**NUTRITION PER SERVING**

Calories **223**  •  Total Fat **11g**  •  Saturated Fat **4g**  •  Cholesterol **197mg**  •  Sodium **626mg**  •

Total Carbohydrate **20g**  •  Dietary Fiber **6g**  •  Sugars **8g**  •  Protein **13g**

# **potato skillet** with eggs + greens

A balanced vegetarian meal featuring eggs that can really be served any time of day. This recipe can easily be scaled up for more people, but makes a splendid one pan meal when cooking for one.

Yield **1 serving**  •  Prep Time **5 minutes**  •  Cook Time **30 minutes**          GF  DF  V  30

1 tsp canola oil

1 medium potato, diced small

¼ tsp kosher salt

Freshly ground black pepper, to taste

2 cups finely chopped kale or Swiss chard

2 large eggs

**1.** Heat the canola oil in a cast-iron skillet over medium heat. Add the potatoes and season with salt and pepper. Sauté for 15 to 20 minutes until the potatoes begin to become tender. Add the kale or chard and sauté for 5 minutes more.

**2.** Push potatoes and greens over to one side of the pan, add eggs to the other side, and cook as desired.

**3.** When eggs are cooked and potatoes are golden brown, transfer to a plate and serve.

**TIP** | Quick cooking hack—place the diced potatoes in a bowl of water and microwave for 5 minutes, drain and pat dry and then add to the pan in step 1.

**NUTRITION PER SERVING**

Calories **363**  •  Total Fat **15g**  •  Saturated Fat **3g**  •  Cholesterol **372mg**  •  Sodium **588mg**  •  Total Carbohydrate **40g**  •  Dietary Fiber **6g**  •  Sugars **3g**  •  Protein **18g**

# skillet gnocchi with tomatoes + swiss chard

Elevate store-bought gnocchi with a few fresh ingredients. This healthier spin on sautéed greens with just the right amount of smoky bacon is sure to make the weeknight dinner hit list.

Yield **4 servings** • Prep Time **5 minutes** • Cook Time **20 minutes**   DF  30

1 (17.5oz) package gnocchi

3 slices bacon, diced

2 tbsp olive oil

1 small onion, diced

2 large tomatoes, diced

1 small bunch Swiss chard, leaves and stems, chopped

¾ tsp kosher salt

Red pepper flakes, to taste

Juice of ½ lemon

1 cup fresh flat-leaf parsley, chopped

**1.** Cook gnocchi in boiling salted water according to package directions. Drain and set aside.

**2.** In a cast-iron skillet, cook the bacon over medium-high heat. Once crisp (about 5 minutes), use a slotted spoon to transfer to a plate lined with paper towel to drain.

**3.** Return the skillet to the stove top over medium-high heat. Add the olive oil followed by the onion, tomatoes, and chard. Sauté until the chard begins to wilt, 2 to 3 minutes. Season with salt, red pepper flakes, and a squeeze of fresh lemon juice.

**4.** Add the cooked bacon and gnocchi to the skillet and continue to cook, tossing gently, for an additional 5 minutes. Top with fresh parsley and serve.

**NUTRITION PER SERVING**
Calories **408** • Total Fat **16g** • Saturated Fat **4g** • Cholesterol **21mg** • Sodium **611mg** •

Total Carbohydrate **41g** • Dietary Fiber **4g** • Sugars **3g** • Protein **16g**

# **egg roll** bowls

Turn a not-so-healthy take-out classic into a healthy and satisfying dinner. Pork is an amazing source of the energy-producing B-vitamin thiamine, and cruciferous veggies like cabbage have cancer-fighting properties.

Yield **6 servings**  •  Prep Time **10 minutes**  •  Cook Time **15 minutes**        DF  30

Canola oil, for frying

10 wonton wrappers

1 lb ground pork

1 small white onion, chopped

2 cloves garlic, minced

2 tsp freshly grated ginger

¼ cup hoisin sauce

1 tbsp reduced-sodium soy sauce

1 head Napa cabbage

1 cup grated carrots

6 cups cooked brown rice, to serve

Sriracha (optional), to serve

**1.** Heat a cast-iron skillet over medium-high heat. Coat the bottom of the pan with canola oil (about ¼ cup).

**2.** Stack the wonton wrappers and cut into ½-inch strips. Once the oil is hot, add the wonton strips and fry in batches until crisp and golden, about 30 seconds per batch. (Use a splatter screen to prevent the oil from splattering, if desired.) Remove from the pan and set aside on a plate lined with paper towel.

**3.** Drain and discard the oil. Return the pan to the stove over medium-high heat. Add the ground pork, onion, garlic, and ginger. Sauté until the pork is browned, about 5 minutes.

**4.** Add the hoisin sauce and soy sauce and continue to cook until pork is cooked through; increase the heat to high for the last few minutes of cooking to develop some caramelization. Add the cabbage and carrots and cook until cabbage is just wilted, 3 to 5 minutes.

**5.** Serve over cooked brown rice, and top with wonton strips and Sriracha, if desired.

**NUTRITION PER SERVING (INCLUDES BROWN RICE)**

Calories **510**  •  Total Fat **18g**  •  Saturated Fat **5g**  •  Cholesterol **45mg**  •  Sodium **420mg**  •

Total Carbohydrate **67g**  •  Dietary Fiber **8g**  •  Sugars **9g**  •  Protein **21g**

# fish tacos
## with kohlrabi slaw

Tacos make the entire family swoon! While I don't make fried fish often, it is always a crowd-pleaser. A crunchy, creamy kohlrabi slaw is the perfect accompaniment to these irresistable tacos.

Yield **4 servings** • Prep Time **20 minutes** • Cook Time **25 minutes**     30

2 cups canola oil

1 lb fresh cod

1 cup all-purpose flour

2 eggs, beaten

2 cups panko bread crumbs

Salt, to taste

8 corn tortillas, warmed, to serve

**For the slaw**

2 tbsp mayonnaise

1 tbsp plain Greek yogurt

Juice of 1 lemon

2 tsp honey

½ tsp celery salt

¼ tsp kosher salt

1 cup grated carrots

2 cups grated kohlrabi

⅛ cup thinly sliced red onion

**1.** In a 12-inch cast-iron skillet, heat the canola oil to 360°F. Use an instant-read thermometer to check that the oil has reached the proper temperature.

**2.** While oil is heating, make the slaw. In a medium bowl, whisk together the mayonnaise, yogurt, lemon juice, honey, celery salt, and kosher salt. Add the carrots, kohlrabi, and onion, and toss to coat with the dressing. Set aside.

**3.** Cut the fish into 16 to 18 evenly sized pieces. Dredge the fish in flour, followed by egg and then panko bread crumbs.

**4.** Working in batches, add the fish to the hot oil and fry for 2 to 3 minutes per side. Then transfer to a plate lined with paper towel and season with salt.

**5.** Serve the fried fish tucked into warmed tortillas and topped with slaw.

**TIP** | Make sure the canola oil is at the proper temperature. This ensures minimal oil absorption, which prevents the fish from getting soggy and keeps the calories and fat in check.

---

**NUTRITION PER SERVING (2 TACOS WITH SLAW)**

Calories **584** • Total Fat **32g** • Saturated Fat **3g** • Cholesterol **109mg** • Sodium **548mg** •
Total Carbohydrate **39g** • Dietary Fiber **5g** • Sugars **10g** • Protein **36g**

# deep dish **pizza**

I am typically a thin crust pizza gal, but making deep dish–style pizza in a cast-iron skillet is a pizza adventure totally worth trying. This recipe follows a classic deep dish method (cheese first, sauce last), but all the ingredients are perfectly portioned to make each slice come in at around 300 calories.

Yield **8 large slices**  •  Prep Time **1 hour 15 minutes (for homemade dough)**  •  Cook Time **20 minutes**

16 oz pizza dough (see Sheet Pan Pizza Night, page 41)

2 oz thinly sliced, nitrate-free salami (Trader Joe's or Applegate brands recommended)

4 oz sliced provolone cheese

1½ cups shredded part-skim mozzarella

1 cup marinara sauce

¼ cup grated Parmesan cheese

**1.** Preheat the oven to 450°F.

**2.** Roll out the pizza dough into a small disc and place in the bottom of a cast iron skillet. Press into the pan so that the dough covers the bottom and rises up the sides by at least 1 inch.

**3.** Arrange the provolone cheese slices as the first layer, followed by shredded mozzarella. Cover the cheese with sliced salami in an even layer. Pour the sauce over top, using a spoon or small spatula to spread it evenly over the salami. Sprinkle with Parmesan cheese.

**4.** Bake for 17 to 20 minutes until the crust is golden brown. Remove from the oven and allow to cool for at least 10 minutes before slicing.

**TIP** | For easy slicing, use a pair of kitchen shears to cut the pizza into wedge slices.

**NUTRITION PER SERVING**

Calories **337**  •  Total Fat **13g**  •  Saturated Fat **6g**  •  Cholesterol **28mg**  •  Sodium **683mg**  •

Total Carbohydrate **37g**  •  Dietary Fiber **2g**  •  Sugars **2g**  •  Protein **17g**

# cast-iron **paella**

Paella is a simple, one-pot crowd-pleaser that looks and tastes exotic. Toss up an arugula salad with a lemony vinaigrette and dinner is done! Make a vegetarian version by substituting extra-firm tofu for the sausage and seafood.

Yield **6 servings**  •  Prep Time **10 minutes**  •  Cook Time **30 minutes**       GF  DF

1 tbsp olive oil

2 links (about 6oz) smoked chorizo chicken sausage (such as Aidells), thinly sliced

⅓ cup chopped onion

3 cloves garlic, minced

1½ cups Arborio rice

1 cup canned diced tomatoes

3 cups low-sodium chicken stock

1 tsp kosher salt

1½ tsp saffron threads

12 oz large shrimp, peeled and deveined

8 oz fresh mussels, scrubbed and rinsed

½ cup chopped fresh parsley, to serve

Lemon wedges, to serve

**1.** In a cast-iron skillet, heat the olive oil over medium-high heat. Add the sausage and cook for 4 to 5 minutes until brown, rendering some of the fat. Remove using a slotted spoon and transfer to a bowl.

**2.** Add the onion and garlic to the hot skillet and sauté until fragrant, about 2 minutes. Add the rice to the skillet and toss to coat with sautéed onions. Add the diced tomatoes, stock, cooked sausage, salt, and saffron, and stir gently. Bring to a simmer, reduce heat to low, cover, and cook for 20 minutes.

**3.** Remove the lid and nestle the shrimp and mussels into the rice. Put the lid back on and continue to cook for 4 more minutes or until the shrimp are opaque and mussels have opened. Sprinkle with parsley and serve with lemon wedges.

**4.** Store leftovers in an airtight container in the refrigerator for up to 4 days.

**TIP** | If you can't find chicken chorizo, use chicken andouille sausage.

**NUTRITION PER SERVING**

Calories **410**  •  Total Fat **10g**  •  Saturated Fat **2g**  •  Cholesterol **122mg**  •  Sodium **664mg**  •

Total Carbohydrate **52g**  •  Dietary Fiber **1g**  •  Sugars **4g**  •  Protein **30g**

**SKILLET**

# simple skillet **lasagna**

This adaptable lasagna is a great way to eat more vegetables, and you can adjust your ingredients with the seasons. Although this is a veggie version, you can add any of your favorite meat fillings to the mix.

Yield **6 servings**  •  Prep Time **7 minutes**  •  Cook Time **20 minutes**     ⓥ 30 FF

2 cups shredded mozzarella

3 tbsp grated Parmesan cheese

1 cup ricotta cheese

1 large egg

Kosher salt and freshly ground black pepper

1¼ cups prepared marinara sauce, divided

6 to 9 no-boil lasagna noodles

3 cups sautéed vegetables such as zucchini, kale, spinach, and onion

Fresh basil, to garnish

**1.** In a small bowl, combine the mozzarella and Parmesan cheese. In a separate bowl, gently mix the ricotta cheese and egg. Season with salt and pepper.

**2.** Heat ½ cup marinara sauce in the bottom of cast-iron skillet over medium-low heat. Add 2 to 3 lasagna noodles, then top with ½ of the vegetables, a few spoonfuls of sauce, ½ of the ricotta mixture, and ⅓ of the mozzarella mixture.

Make the next layer with 2 to 3 more noodles, remaining vegetables, a few more spoonfuls of sauce, the remaining ricotta mixture, and an additional ⅓ of the mozzarella mixture.

**3.** For the final layer, use the remaining noodles, followed by the remaining sauce and mozzarella mixture.

**4.** Cover and cook for 20 minutes, or until cheese is melted and noodles are tender. Allow to cool slightly and garnish with fresh basil before serving.

**5.** Leftovers can be stored in an airtight container in the refrigerator for 5 days or frozen for up to 3 months.

**VARIATION** | To make gluten-free, substitute gluten-free lasagna noodles.

---

**NUTRITION PER SERVING**

62    Calories **309**  •  Total Fat **17g**  •  Saturated Fat **9g**  •  Cholesterol **76mg**  •  Sodium **718mg**  •
Total Carbohydrate **21g**  •  Dietary Fiber **2g**  •  Sugars **5g**  •  Protein **20g**

# skirt steak with chimichurri

You can make restaurant-quality steak in your kitchen—the secret weapon is your cast-iron skillet. A quick sear and this steak is done. Whip up an herbaceous sauce for a dose of antioxidants and healthy fats, and serve with a salad or a warm loaf of crusty whole-grain bread.

Yield **6 servings**  •  Prep Time **10 minutes**  •  Cook Time **12 minutes**

2 lb skirt steak (2 to 3 pieces)

½ tsp kosher salt

½ tsp freshly ground black pepper

**For the chimichurri**

2 cloves garlic

2 cups fresh cilantro (leaves and stems)

2 cups fresh parsley (leaves and stems)

3 scallions, roughly chopped

1 small jalapeño pepper

Zest and juice of 1 lime

¼ cup rice wine vinegar

¾ tsp kosher salt

¾ cup olive oil

1. Heat a cast-iron skillet over high heat, and season the steak with salt and pepper on both sides. Once the skillet is hot, add the steak and cook for 5 to 6 minutes per side, or until meat is cooked to desired doneness.

2. While the steak is cooking, prepare the chimichurri. Place the garlic in a food processor and pulse until chopped. Add the cilantro, parsley, scallions, jalapeño, lime, vinegar, and salt, and process again until all ingredients are well combined. Transfer to a medium bowl and whisk in the olive oil.

3. When the steak is cooked, remove from the skillet and place on a cutting board to rest for 5 to 10 minutes. Slice and serve with chimichurri spooned over the top.

4. Leftover chimichurri can be stored in an airtight container in the refrigerator for up to 1 week.

**TIP** | Skirt steak is an amazing source of iron, a mineral most women need more of.

**NUTRITION PER SERVING**

Calories **427**  •  Total Fat **34g**  •  Saturated Fat **10g**  •  Cholesterol **104mg**  •  Sodium **309mg**  •

Total Carbohydrate **2g**  •  Dietary Fiber **2g**  •  Sugars **0g**  •  Protein **30g**

# skillet **chicken sausage + peppers**

This lightened-up version of the Italian classic is quick cooking and crowd pleasing. Lower fat chicken sausage has all the flavor of regular pork sausage and is higher in protein. Serve on whole-grain rolls or with brown rice.

Yield **4 servings** • Prep Time **5 minutes** • Cook Time **15 minutes**     GF DF 30 FF

1 tbsp olive oil

1 lb chicken sausage, sliced (Aidells brand recommended)

1 clove garlic, finely chopped

1 red onion, sliced

2 bell peppers, any color, cut into strips

¼ tsp kosher salt

¼ tsp freshly ground black pepper

2 tsp Worcestershire sauce

1 tbsp tomato paste

¼ cup chicken stock or water

1 tsp chopped fresh thyme leaves

¼ cup chopped fresh basil, to garnish

**1.** In a large skillet, heat the olive oil over medium-high heat. Add the sausage, garlic, onion, and peppers and cook for 2 to 3 minutes. Season with salt and pepper and cook for 5 minutes more.

**2.** Add the Worcestershire, tomato paste, chicken stock, and thyme. Continue to cook for an additional 5 minutes or until sausage is heated through and vegetables are tender. Garnish with fresh basil and serve.

**3.** Store leftovers in an airtight container in the refrigerator for 3 to 4 days or freeze for up to 3 months.

---

**NUTRITION PER SERVING (DOES NOT INCLUDE ROLLS OR RICE)**

Calories **168** • Total Fat **10g** • Saturated Fat **3g** • Cholesterol **55mg** • Sodium **416mg** •
Total Carbohydrate **11g** • Dietary Fiber **3g** • Sugars **5g** • Protein **12g**

# **cheeseburger** sliders

Think of your cast-iron skillet as a mini version of the well-seasoned grill at that diner with the burgers you love. Lean ground beef not only provides muscle-building protein and iron, but also energy-producing B vitamins. Pile high with your favorite toppings and serve with sweet potato fries.

Yield **6 burgers** • Prep Time **10 minutes** • Cook Time **20 minutes**      **30** **FF**

---

1½ lb 90% lean ground beef

3 tbsp grated yellow onion

Kosher salt and freshly ground black pepper

3 oz cheese, cut into 6 slices

6 small dinner rolls

**1.** In a medium bowl, use your hands to combine the ground beef and onion. Form into the mixture into 6 burger patties and season both sides of each patty with salt and pepper.

**2.** Heat a cast-iron skillet over medium-high heat. Working in batches, add the burger patties to the skillet and cook for 4 to 6 minutes per side or to your desired doneness. Add cheese for the last 2 minutes of cooking. Serve on rolls with your favorite toppings.

**3.** Freeze raw or cooked burgers in a freezer-safe bag for up to 3 months. Defrost raw burgers in the fridge overnight before cooking. Cooked burgers can be reheated in the microwave

**TIP** | To make sweet potato fries, peel and evenly slice 2 to 3 medium sweet potatoes. Toss with olive oil, salt, and pepper and bake or air fry at 375°F until crisp, about 30 minutes.

---

**NUTRITION PER BURGER**

Calories **315** • Total Fat **14g** • Saturated Fat **5.5g** • Cholesterol **81mg** • Sodium **495mg** • Total Carbohydrate **15g** • Dietary Fiber **1g** • Sugars **2g** • Protein **27g**

# lemon-thyme dutch baby
## with smoked salmon

This savory pancake is a dinner (or brunch) winner. Watch it get puffed and golden in the oven and top with pieces of delicate smoked salmon for a protein boost.

Yield **4 servings** • Prep Time **10 minutes** • Cook Time **20 minutes**

1 tbsp chopped fresh thyme

Zest of ½ lemon

¼ cup grated Parmesan cheese

4 tbsp unsalted butter, divided

4 large eggs (at room temperature)

½ cup whole milk

½ cup flour

Salt and freshly ground black pepper

4 oz smoked salmon

**1.** Preheat the oven to 450°F. In a small bowl, combine the thyme, lemon zest, and Parmesan cheese. Mix and set aside.

**2.** Place 2 tablespoons butter in a cast-iron skillet. Put the skillet in the oven for 2 minutes or until butter is melted. Carefully remove the hot skillet from the oven, swirl to fully coat the bottom with melted butter, and set aside.

**3.** In a separate small saucepan, melt the remaining 2 tablespoons butter. In a blender, combine the melted butter, eggs, milk, flour, salt, and pepper. Blend until smooth.

**4.** Pour the batter into the hot skillet. Sprinkle with the Parmesan mixture. Return to the oven and bake for 20 minutes or until puffed and golden.

**5.** Remove from the oven and top with smoked salmon before serving.

**VARIATION** | For an extra protein boost, add a fried egg on top.

**NUTRITION PER SERVING**

Calories **357** • Total Fat **21g** • Saturated Fat **9g** • Cholesterol **220mg** • Sodium **986mg** •

Total Carbohydrate **14g** • Dietary Fiber **0.5g** • Sugars **2g** • Protein **26g**

# **steak** caesar salad

Caesar salad can fall short of gourmet fare when it's nothing but a pile of lettuce with cheese and gloppy dressing. Give this classic salad a healthy upgrade with extra veggies, homemade dressing, and (drum roll, please) filet mignon.

Yield **2 servings** • Prep Time **5 minutes** • Cook Time **15 minutes, plus 10 minutes to rest**

2 tsp olive oil

2 oz day-old bread (preferably whole-grain), cubed

1 tsp kosher salt

½ tsp freshly ground black pepper

2 (6oz) filet mignon

2 romaine hearts, sliced

1 pt cherry tomatoes, halved

¼ cup shredded Parmesan cheese

**For the dressing**

2 tbsp olive oil

2 tbsp freshly squeezed lemon juice

1 tsp Dijon mustard

Dash of Worcestershire sauce

2 tbsp grated Parmesan cheese

½ tsp minced garlic

2 tsp mayonnaise

½ tsp anchovy paste

Freshly ground black pepper, to taste

**1.** In a cast iron skillet, heat the olive oil over medium heat. Add the bread cubes to the pan, season with a pinch of salt and pepper, and sauté until well toasted. Remove from pan and set croutons aside.

**2.** Wipe out the skillet to remove any crumbs, return to the stove top, and increase heat to high. Preheat the oven to 400°F.

**3.** Season the steaks generously on both sides with salt and pepper. Place the steaks in the hot skillet and sear for 2 minutes per side.

**4.** Transfer the skillet to the preheated oven and cook for an additional 4 to 5 minutes or until the steak is cooked as desired. Allow to rest for 10 minutes before slicing.

**5.** While the steak rests, make the dressing. In a small bowl, combine the olive oil, lemon juice, mustard, Worcestershire, Parmesan cheese, garlic, mayonnaise, anchovy paste, and pepper. Whisk well.

**6.** Slice the steak and serve with romaine topped with cherry tomatoes, toasted croutons, Parmesan cheese, and Caesar dressing.

**VARIATION** | Like a grilled salad? Place romaine hearts in a hot skillet, cut-side down to heat up the lettuce and give it a little bit of charred flavor.

**NUTRITION PER SERVING**

Calories **593** • Total Fat **25g** • Saturated Fat **7g** • Cholesterol **82mg** • Sodium **713mg** •

Total Carbohydrate **42g** • Dietary Fiber **4g** • Sugars **12g** • Protein **45g**

# kitchen sink **fried rice**

This is my go-to dinner when I've got all kinds of leftovers on hand. You can use just about any protein and veggie combination and end up with a super quick and tasty meal. It's the perfect dish for cleaning out the fridge or freezer.

Yield **4 servings**  •  Prep Time **8 minutes**  •  Cook Time **15 minutes**    DF  30

2 tsp sesame oil

¼ cup low-sodium soy sauce or gluten-free tamari

2 tbsp rice vinegar

1 tbsp granulated sugar

2 tsp cornstarch

2 tbsp canola oil, divided

1 large egg, beaten

2 cloves garlic, chopped

6 oz protein (cooked shrimp, chicken, beef, tofu, or edamame)

3 cups chopped fresh vegetables (such as broccoli, peppers, carrots, green beans, or mushrooms)

4 cups cooked brown rice

Cashews, chopped, to serve

1. In a small bowl, whisk together sesame oil, soy sauce, vinegar, sugar, and cornstarch. Set aside.

2. In a large skillet or wok, heat 1 tablespoon canola oil over high heat. Add the egg and gently scramble; remove egg from pan and set aside.

3. Return the skillet to the stove top. Heat the remaining 1 tablespoon canola oil, add the garlic, and sauté 1 to 2 minutes until fragrant. Add the protein and vegetables, and cook for 2 to 3 minutes more.

4. Add the sauce and cook for 2 minutes more or until the vegetables reach desired doneness. Add the rice and scrambled egg. Continue to cook, stirring frequently, until all ingredients are heated through, about 5 minutes.

5. Top with cashews and serve. Store leftovers in the refrigerator in an airtight container for up to 4 days.

**TIP** | Save yourself prep time and use frozen veggies, which are a great option in the winter months when so many vegetables are out of season.

**NUTRITION PER SERVING**

Calories **412**  •  Total Fat **14g**  •  Saturated Fat **2g**  •  Cholesterol **71mg**  •  Sodium **848mg**  •  Total Carbohydrate **60g**  •  Dietary Fiber **6g**  •  Sugars **3g**  •  Protein **19g**

# baked **stuffed zucchini**

A deliciously easy main course featuring this garden-fresh favorite! Looking for something new to do with all of that zucchini? Here you go! Need more convincing? This summer squash is high in water and fiber, and contains antioxidants with anti-inflammatory properties.

Yield **4 servings**  •  Prep Time **10 minutes**  •  Cook Time **40 minutes**          GF

2 large (or 4 small) zucchini

2 tbsp olive oil, divided

1 tsp kosher salt, divided

Freshly ground black pepper

1 lb lean ground beef

1 clove garlic, minced

½ onion, chopped

1 bell pepper, chopped

2 cups chopped kale

¾ cup marinara sauce

1 cup shredded part-skim mozzarella

**1.** Preheat the oven to 350°F. Cut the zucchini in half lengthwise. Using a spoon, scoop out the seeded flesh (you can also use a melon baller) and set aside.

**2.** Place the zucchini shells on a sheet pan, cut-side up. Drizzle with 1 tablespoon olive oil and season with ½ tsp salt and pepper. (If the zucchini tips over, gently cut away a thin slice from the bottom to help it lie flat.) Set aside.

**3.** In a large skillet, heat the remaining 1 tablespoon olive oil over medium-high heat. Add the ground beef, season with ½ tsp salt and pepper, and cook for 5 minutes or until browned. Add the reserved zucchini flesh along with the garlic, onion, and bell pepper. Sauté for 2 to 3 minutes. Add the kale and marinara sauce and cook for 5 to 7 minutes more or until veggies are tender.

**4.** Fill the zucchini with the meat mixture and top with mozzarella. Bake for 20 to 25 minutes, until the cheese is bubbly and zucchini is tender.

**TIP** | If the cheese begins to brown before the zucchini is cooked, cover loosely with aluminum foil and continue to bake.

**VARIATION** | Make with lean ground turkey or for a vegetarian version, cooked lentils.

**NUTRITION PER SERVING**

Calories **392**  •  Total Fat **24g**  •  Saturated Fat **8g**  •  Cholesterol **90mg**  •  Sodium **373mg**  •

Total Carbohydrate **14g**  •  Dietary Fiber **3g**  •  Sugars **7g**  •  Protein **31g**

gluten-free **GF**
dairy-free **DF**
vegan **V**
under 30 minutes **30**
freezer friendly **FF**

# dutch oven

# shepherd's pie

This hearty dish is one of the very best meals for a chilly evening, upgraded with extra veggies. Less meat and more mushrooms result in a dish that's lighter and more flavorful than the traditional version.

Yield **6 servings** • Prep Time **10 minutes** • Cook Time **45 minutes**

1 lb potatoes, peeled and diced

2¾ tsp kosher salt, divided

½ cup low-fat milk

4 tbsp unsalted butter, divided

1 lb 90% lean ground beef

1 onion, chopped

1 green bell pepper, chopped

2 cups sliced mushrooms

2 tbsp tomato paste

1 tbsp all-purpose flour

¾ cup vegetable, beef, or chicken broth

1 cup corn kernels (fresh or frozen)

**1.** Place the potatoes in a 4½-quart Dutch oven and add cold water to cover. Bring to a boil over high heat, add 2 teaspoons salt, reduce heat, and simmer for 15 minutes or until potatoes are tender. Drain. Transfer the potatoes to a large bowl, add milk and 2 tablespoons butter, season with ½ teaspoon salt and mash until smooth. Set aside.

**2.** Preheat the oven to 350°F. Return the pot to the stove top over medium heat. Add the ground beef and sauté for 6 to 7 minutes until brown.

**3.** Add the onion, bell pepper, mushrooms, and tomato paste. Season with the remaining ¼ teaspoon salt and cook for 5 minutes to allow the vegetables to become tender. Sprinkle with flour and cook for 2 to 3 minutes, then pour in the broth and allow to thicken, 2 to 3 minutes more.

**4.** Remove the pot from the heat. Add the corn in a layer over the beef and then spread mashed potatoes over the top. Cut the remaining 2 tablespoons butter into small pieces and dot over the top of the potatoes. Place in the oven and bake for 20 minutes. Allow to cool slightly before serving.

**5.** Store leftovers in an airtight container in the refrigerator for 3 to 4 days or in the freezer for up to 3 months.

**TIP** | Try using sweet potatoes or turnips for the topping in place of regular potatoes. You can also try any seasonal vegetable in the filling.

---

**NUTRITION PER SERVING**

Calories **459** • Total Fat **22g** • Saturated Fat **11g** • Cholesterol **104mg** • Sodium **743mg** •
Total Carbohydrate **36g** • Dietary Fiber **5.5g** • Sugars **8g** • Protein **30g**

# **quesadilla** lasagna

Enjoy a Mexican spin on a classic Italian dinner. With layers of lean ground turkey, sautéed veggies, and melted cheese sandwiched between whole-grain tortillas, this dish will definitely be a weeknight dinner favorite.

Yield **4 servings**  •  Prep Time **12 minutes**  •  Cook Time **20 minutes**    **30**  **FF**

1 tsp olive oil

1 lb ground turkey breast

½ red onion, finely chopped

1 clove garlic, minced

Salt and freshly ground black pepper, to taste

1 tsp ground cumin

1 tsp chili powder

1 small zucchini, sliced

1 yellow bell pepper, chopped

1 jalapeño pepper, minced (optional)

3 (8-inch) whole-wheat flour tortillas

1 cup shredded low-fat cheddar cheese, divided

¾ cup salsa, divided

1 avocado, diced

**1.** Preheat the oven to 375°F. In a 4½-quart Dutch oven, heat the olive oil over medium heat. Once hot, add the ground turkey and sauté for 4 to 5 minutes until browned.

**2.** Add the onion and garlic and cook for an additional 2 minutes. Season with salt, pepper, cumin, and chili powder; stir to combine. Add the zucchini, bell pepper, and jalapeño and cook, stirring continuously, until turkey meat is no longer pink and vegetables are slightly tender.

**3.** Turn off the heat and transfer the mixture to a plate. Wipe out the Dutch oven and spray with nonstick cooking spray.

**4.** Place 1 tortilla on the bottom of the pot. Top with ½ of the turkey mixture and ¼ cup cheese. Create second layer with another tortilla, and add the remaining turkey mixture and another ¼ cup cheese. Create top layer with remaining tortilla, ¼ cup salsa, and the remaining ½ cup cheese. Bake until the cheese is melted, about 15 minutes.

**5.** In a small bowl, combine the diced avocado with the remaining ½ cup salsa.

**6.** Slice the lasagna and serve topped with salsa-avocado mixture. Store leftovers in an airtight container in the refrigerator for 3 to 4 days or in the freezer for up to 3 months.

**VARIATION** | To make gluten-free, use gluten-free tortillas.
To make vegetarian, replace the turkey with 1 (15oz) can black beans.

**NUTRITION PER SERVING**

Calories **437**  •  Total Fat **15g**  •  Saturated Fat **2g**  •  Cholesterol **77mg**  •  Sodium **892mg**  •

Total Carbohydrate **42g**  •  Dietary Fiber **16g**  •  Sugars **3g**  •  Protein **47g**

# one-pot
# lemony caprese linguine

You won't believe this recipe until you try it for yourself. A one-and-done pasta dish with all the fresh flavors of summer. It's a little-known fact that fresh mozzarella adds plenty of protein.

Yield **4 servings**  •  Prep Time **5 minutes**  •  Cook Time **10 minutes**          V

12 oz linguine fini

1 tbsp olive oil

2 tsp kosher salt

½ lemon, thinly sliced

2 cloves garlic, sliced

1 medium tomato, diced

1 cup basil leaves, chopped

½ cup grated Parmesan cheese

6 oz fresh mozzarella, diced

Red pepper flakes (optional), to serve

**1.** Place the pasta, olive oil, salt, lemon, and garlic in a large (5½- to 7¼-quart) Dutch oven and cover with 4¼ cups water.

**2.** Bring to a boil over medium-high heat. As soon as the pasta begins to soften, stir frequently for 8 to 10 minutes until the pasta is al dente and the liquid is fully absorbed.

**3.** Top with the tomato, basil, Parmesan, and mozzarella. Serve immediately with red pepper flakes, if desired.

**TIP** | Linguine fini is a thinner cut of linguine. You can also use regular linguine or spaghetti, but you will need to adjust the cook time according to package directions and may need a few extra splashes of water.

**NUTRITION PER SERVING**

Calories **542**  •  Total Fat **18g**  •  Saturated Fat **8g**  •  Cholesterol **36mg**  •  Sodium **696mg**  •
Total Carbohydrate **63g**  •  Dietary Fiber **3g**  •  Sugars **3g**  •  Protein **26g**

# balsamic braised
# **chicken thighs**

File chicken thighs as one of the most underappreciated protein sources around. This "dark" meat is actually filled with iron and heart-healthy polyunsaturated fats, which makes them super flavorful and prevents them from drying out.

Yield **4 servings** • Prep Time **10 minutes** • Cook Time **30 minutes**     GF  DF

2 tsp olive oil

8 bone-in, skin-on chicken thighs

1 tsp kosher salt

½ tsp freshly ground black pepper

2 onions, sliced

3 bell peppers, any color, sliced

¼ cup balsamic vinegar

2 tsp honey

**1.** In a large (5½- to 7¼-quart) Dutch oven, heat the olive oil over medium-high heat. Season the chicken thighs with salt and pepper and place in the pot skin-side down. (If the chicken thighs are large, do this in two batches so you don't overcrowd the pan.) Sear for 5 to 6 minutes and then transfer to a plate.

**2.** Return the pot to the stove top over medium-high heat. Add the peppers and onions and toss to coat with the chicken drippings. Add the vinegar and honey and toss to combine.

**3.** Add the chicken back to the pot on top of the vegetables and reduce the heat to low. Partially cover and cook for 20 minutes or until the chicken reaches an internal temperature of 165°F.

**TIP** | The saturated fat in chicken thighs is mostly in the skin, which can be removed after cooking, if desired.

**NUTRITION PER SERVING (2 CHICKEN THIGHS)**

Calories **402** • Total Fat **21g** • Saturated Fat **5.5g** • Cholesterol **114mg** • Sodium **583mg** •

Total Carbohydrate **15g** • Dietary Fiber **2.5g** • Sugars **9g** • Protein **33g**

# butternut squash soup
## with beans + escarole

Escarole is a leafy green veggie that's filled with fiber. It has a slightly bitter taste, which is the perfect balance to naturally sweet butternut squash. This soul-soothing soup makes for a cozy dinner on a chilly fall evening.

Yield **4 servings** • Prep Time **10 minutes** • Cook Time **30 minutes**    GF DF FF

3 tbsp olive oil, divided

1 small head escarole, chopped

3 cloves garlic, chopped

1 onion, chopped

2 tsp fresh thyme leaves

1½ tsp kosher salt

Freshly ground black pepper

1 (15oz) can diced tomatoes

1 medium butternut squash, peeled and diced

4 cups low-sodium chicken broth

2 tsp balsamic vinegar

1 (15oz) can cannellini beans, drained and rinsed

**1.** In a large (5½- to 7¼-quart) Dutch oven, heat 1 tablespoon olive oil over medium-high heat. Add the escarole and garlic and sauté until greens are just wilted, about 5 minutes. Remove from pot and set aside.

**2.** Return the pot to the stove top, reduce the heat to medium, and heat remaining 2 tablespoons olive oil. Add the onion and thyme and season with salt and pepper to taste. Cook for 5 minutes to soften the onion. Stir in the tomatoes, squash, and broth. Bring soup to a simmer and cook for 20 minutes or until the squash is tender.

**3.** Purée the soup in a blender (in batches), or leave in the pot and use an immersion blender. Stir in the vinegar, cooked greens, and beans. Heat for an additional 5 minutes to warm the beans before serving.

**4.** Store leftovers in an airtight container in the refrigerator for up to 4 days or freeze for up to 3 months.

**TIP** | Replace the raw squash in this recipe with leftover roasted squash or even canned squash purée. If the squash is already cooked, the simmering time can be reduced.

**VARIATION** | To make vegetarian, use vegetable broth.

**NUTRITION PER SERVING**

Calories **377** • Total Fat **12g** • Saturated Fat **2g** • Cholesterol **0mg** • Sodium **605mg** •

Total Carbohydrate **59g** • Dietary Fiber **12g** • Sugars **10g** • Protein **16g**

# lightened-up **new england clam chowder**

In its traditional form, this creamy seafood chowder can be a belly buster. This one-pot recipe has all the classic flavors (even bacon), but it's made with a few lighter swaps, so you get all the goodness with none of the guilt.

Yield **6 servings**  •  Prep Time **15 minutes**  •  Cook Time **35 minutes**           FF

2 slices thick-cut bacon, chopped (Applegate brand recommended)

1 tbsp olive oil

1 tbsp unsalted butter

1 yellow onion, chopped

3 medium carrots, chopped

3 medium celery stalks, chopped

1 clove garlic, minced

1 tbsp chopped fresh thyme leaves

1 tsp kosher salt

½ tsp freshly ground black pepper

2 tbsp all-purpose flour

2 medium russet potatoes, peeled and diced

3 cups clam juice

2 cups whole milk, warmed

4 oz chopped clams

Oyster crackers (optional), to serve

**1.** In a large (5½- to 7¼-quart) Dutch oven, cook the bacon over medium-high heat until the fat is rendered and the bacon is crispy. Remove using a slotted spoon and transfer to a plate lined with paper towel.

**2.** Add the olive oil and butter to the pot, followed by the onion, carrot, and celery. Cook for 3 to 4 minutes until the vegetables become tender. Add the garlic, thyme, salt, and pepper, and cook for 2 minutes more.

**3.** Sprinkle the flour into the pot and stir. Cook for 2 minutes and then add the potatoes and clam juice to the pot.

**4.** Bring the soup to a boil and then reduce to a simmer; cook for 20 minutes. Stir in the reserved bacon, warm milk, and clams. Bring the soup back to a simmer and cook for 5 minutes more until clams are fully cooked.

**5.** Serve hot or cool with oyster crackers, if desired. Store in an airtight container for up to 4 days in the refrigerator or freeze for up to 3 months.

**TIP** | Look for fresh or frozen wild chopped clams.

**VARIATION** | For a vegetarian corn chowder, swap vegetable broth for clam juice, omit the clams, and substitute with corn kernels.

**NUTRITION PER SERVING**

Calories **217**  •  Total Fat **9g**  •  Saturated Fat **4g**  •  Cholesterol **30mg**  •  Sodium **574mg**  •

Total Carbohydrate **25g**  •  Dietary Fiber **3g**  •  Sugars **8g**  •  Protein **10g**

# pumpkin + turnip soup
# with turmeric

When my daughter was home with a cold, I wanted to make something to help her. While there is no such thing as a cure for a cold, this is pretty close— made with antioxidant-rich vegetables and inflammation-fighting turmeric.

Yield **4 servings**  •  Prep Time **10 minutes**  •  Cook Time **25 minutes**       GF DF V 30

2 tbsp olive oil

1 medium butternut squash, peeled, seeded, and diced

3 medium turnips, peeled and diced

1 tsp kosher salt

½ tsp freshly ground black pepper

3 cloves garlic, chopped

1 tbsp chopped fresh oregano

2 tsp chopped fresh thyme

5 cups low-sodium vegetable stock or chicken stock

1 (15oz) can pumpkin purée

1 tbsp ground turmeric

**1.** In a large (5½- to 7¼-quart) Dutch oven, heat the olive oil over medium-high heat. Add the squash and turnips and season with salt and pepper.

**2.** Add the garlic, oregano, thyme, and chicken stock. Bring to a boil, then reduce heat to a simmer, partially cover, and cook for 20 minutes or until the vegetables are tender.

**3.** Stir in the pumpkin and turmeric. Using an immersion blender, purée until smooth. Taste for seasoning and serve.

**TIP** | For a crunchy topping (and protein boost) add some baked chickpeas!

**VARIATION** | Instead of boiling, roast the vegetables and herbs on a sheet pan. Then add to a pot with stock and blend.

**NUTRITION PER SERVING**

82  Calories **192**  •  Total Fat **8g**  •  Saturated Fat **1g**  •  Cholesterol **0mg**  •  Sodium **596mg**  •  Total Carbohydrate **30g**  •  Dietary Fiber **7g**  •  Sugars **9g**  •  Protein **4g**

# jambalaya pasta

A classic rice dish gets new life with whole-grain pasta. This spicy one-pot dinner will please hungry kids on a weeknight, but can also be made for company on a chilly fall game day. Chicken andouille sausage and chicken breast makes this version much lighter than the traditional dish.

Yield **6 servings**  •  Prep Time **10 minutes**  •  Cook Time **30 minutes**

1 lb whole-wheat penne

2 fully cooked andouille chicken sausages (Aidells brand recommended), sliced

4 oz chicken breast, thinly sliced

1 medium onion, diced

1 green bell pepper, diced

2 cloves garlic, finely chopped

½ tsp kosher salt

8 oz tomato sauce

1 cup low-sodium chicken stock

2 tsp hot sauce

Scallions, chopped, to garnish

Fresh basil, chopped, to garnish

**1.** In a large (5½- to 7¼-quart) Dutch oven, cook the pasta according to package directions; drain and set aside.

**2.** Return the Dutch oven to the stove top over medium-high heat. Add the sausage and sauté until browned, 2 to 3 minutes. Remove using a slotted spoon and set aside in a bowl.

**3.** Add the chicken to the pot and cook for 5 minutes, turning once.  Add the onion, pepper and garlic. Season with salt and sauté for 5 minutes more.

**4.** Add the tomato sauce, chicken stock, and hot sauce, and bring the mixture to a boil. Reduce to a simmer and cook for 5 minutes. Add pasta and cooked sausage back to the pot and toss to combine. Serve topped with chopped scallions and basil.

---

**NUTRITION PER SERVING**

Calories **504**  •  Total Fat **11g**  •  Saturated Fat **2.5g**  •  Cholesterol **103mg**  •  Sodium **789mg**  •
Total Carbohydrate **59g**  •  Dietary Fiber **9g**  •  Sugars **3g**  •  Protein **46g**

# sweet + spicy **lamb tagine**

The spices in this Moroccan-inspired recipe are potent inflammation-fighting and cell-protecting antioxidants. If you aren't used to cooking lamb, this easy Dutch oven recipe is a great way to get started.

Yield **6 servings**  •  Prep Time **15 minutes**  •  Cook Time **1 hour 15 minutes**

2 lb bone-in lamb stew meat

1 tsp kosher salt

½ tsp freshly ground black pepper

1 tbsp olive oil

2 cloves garlic, chopped

1 small onion, chopped

2 tsp minced fresh ginger

1 tsp ground cumin

1 tsp ground turmeric

½ tsp ground allspice

¼ tsp cayenne

1 cinnamon stick

½ cup low-sodium chicken stock

1 cup canned diced tomatoes

½ cup dried apricots, chopped

1 (15oz) can chickpeas, drained and rinsed

½ cup shelled pistachios, roughly chopped

½ cup chopped fresh parsley

6 cups cooked couscous, to serve (see tip)

1. Preheat the oven to 350°F.

2. Season the lamb with salt and pepper. In a large (5½- to 7¼-quart) Dutch oven, heat the olive oil over medium heat. Once hot, add the lamb and brown on both sides, about 5 to 6 minutes per side. Remove the lamb from the pan and transfer to a plate.

3. Add the garlic, onion, ginger, cumin, turmeric, allspice, cayenne, and cinnamon stick to the pot. Sauté for 2 to 3 minutes and then add the chicken stock to deglaze the pan, scraping up any brown bits from the bottom of the Dutch oven.

4. Stir in the tomatoes and apricots and then return the lamb to the pot. Cover and place in the oven for 1 hour.

5. When the cook time is up, carefully remove the pot from the oven, remove the lid, remove the cinnamon stick, and stir in the chickpeas. Taste for seasoning and add additional salt if desired. Top with pistachios and parsley and serve with couscous.

6. If freezing, do not add pistachios. Once cooled, transfer to an airtight container and freeze for up to 3 months.

**TIP** | To prepare couscous, place 1½ cups dry couscous in a bowl and add 2 cups boiling water or chicken broth. Stir, cover with plastic wrap, and allow to sit for 5 minutes. Stir in ¼ cup chopped parsley, if desired, fluff with a fork, and serve.

---

**NUTRITION PER SERVING**

Calories **585**  •  Total Fat **28g**  •  Saturated Fat **11g**  •  Cholesterol **87mg**  •  Sodium **415mg**  •
Total Carbohydrate **52g**  •  Dietary Fiber **7g**  •  Sugars **7g**  •  Protein **32g**

# everything bagel **muffaletta**

The best-kept secret recipe using a Dutch oven is no-knead bread. While this recipe does require some pre-planning, it's worth every second. This New Orleans classic sandwich has it all—layers of spicy meats and cheese, topped with a briny olive salad. This lightened-up version doesn't disappoint.

Yield **4 servings**  •  Prep Time **20 minutes, plus 8–12 hours inactive time**  •  Cook Time **45 minutes**

1 tsp dry active yeast

½ tsp honey

1½ tsp kosher salt

3 cups all-purpose flour

2 tbsp olive oil

Everything bagel seasoning

**For the sandwiches**

⅓ cup finely chopped black olives

⅓ cup finely chopped green olives

2 tbsp minced carrot

1 clove garlic, minced

1 tbsp balsamic vinegar

3 tbsp olive oil

3 slices provolone cheese

2 oz thinly sliced turkey breast

2 oz thinly sliced Genoa salami (Applegate brand recommended)

1. To make the bread, combine the yeast, honey, and ¼ cup water in a large bowl. Stir and wait 5 minutes for bubbles to form. Add the salt, flour, and 1¼ cups water. Mix well with a spatula until a loose dough forms. Cover with plastic wrap and allow to rest for 8 to 12 hours.

2. Place a large (5½- to 7¼-quart) Dutch oven in the oven and preheat to 450°F for 25 minutes.

3. Remove the plastic wrap and punch down the dough. Turn out onto a piece of parchment paper dusted with flour. (It will be sticky!) Shape the dough into a ball and allow to rest while the oven heats.

4. Carefully remove the Dutch oven and remove lid. Using parchment paper, lower the dough into the bottom of the pot. Cover and return to the oven to bake for 30 minutes.

5. Remove the lid, brush with olive oil, and sprinkle with everything bagel seasoning. Bake uncovered for 5 to 10 minutes more until top is golden brown. Remove from the oven and allow to cool for at least 10 minutes before removing the loaf from the pot and transferring to a wire rack to cool.

6. To build the sandwiches, slice the loaf in half lengthwise and place each half cut-side up on a sheet pan. Place in a 350°F oven for 10 minutes to toast.

7. Meanwhile, in a small bowl, mix together the black and green olives, carrot, garlic, vinegar, and olive oil.

8. Remove the bread from the oven and layer the cheese and meats on the bottom half of the loaf; top with the olive mixture. Replace the top half of the loaf and press down. Using a serrated knife, cut into 4 pieces.

**TIP** | The bread can be made a day ahead and stored on the countertop, or wrapped tightly in plastic wrap and stored in the freezer for up to 3 months.

**NUTRITION PER SERVING**

Calories **545**  •  Total Fat **16.5g**  •  Saturated Fat **6g**  •  Cholesterol **35mg**  •  Sodium **911mg**  •  Total Carbohydrate **75g**  •  Dietary Fiber **4g**  •  Sugars **3g**  •  Protein **21g**

# baked **pasta primavera**

Pasta can make for the ultimate healthy vegetarian meal when loaded with vegetables and low-fat cheese. The key is portion control. One pound of pasta is appropriate for six people, not four people, as many recipes specify.

Yield **6 servings**  •  Prep Time **10 minutes**  •  Cook Time **30 minutes**

1 lb penne or other tubular pasta

2 tbsp prepared pesto (or make your own; see tip)

¼ cup heavy cream

1 pt cherry tomatoes, halved

6 oz baby spinach

1 cup shredded part-skim mozzarella

**1.** Cook the pasta in a large (5½- to 7¼-quart) Dutch oven according to package directions; drain and set aside.

**2.** Return the Dutch oven to the stove top over medium-high heat. Preheat the broiler to high.

**3.** Add the pesto and cream to the pot, stir, and bring to a simmer. Add the tomatoes, spinach, and cooked pasta, and mix to combine. Sprinkle with cheese and transfer to the broiler.

**4.** Broil for 1 to 2 minutes until the cheese is melted and bubbly. Carefully remove from the oven and serve.

**5.** Store leftovers in an airtight container in the refrigerator for up to 4 days. To freeze, allow to cool to room temperature and transfer to a freezer-safe container. Freeze for up to 3 months.

**TIP** | Make your own pesto by combining fresh basil, garlic, lemon juice, toasted pine nuts or walnuts (or no nuts), salt, and pepper in a food processor. With the machine running, pour in olive oil until the sauce reaches desired consistency.

---

**NUTRITION PER SERVING**

Calories **405**  •  Total Fat **14g**  •  Saturated Fat **6g**  •  Cholesterol **96mg**  •  Sodium **301mg**  •

Total Carbohydrate **52g**  •  Dietary Fiber **2g**  •  Sugars **2g**  •  Protein **20g**

# **seafood** bouillabaisse

This seafood stew is loaded with fish and shellfish in a savory, saffron-infused tomato broth. Light but filling, it's a scrumptious way to get everyone in your house to eat more seafood. Serve with crusty bread to sop up every drop.

Yield **6 servings** • Prep Time **15 minutes** • Cook Time **45 minutes**

2 tbsp olive oil

½ yellow onion, chopped

1 bulb fennel, chopped, reserving some of the leafy green fronds

3 cloves garlic, chopped

1 tsp kosher salt

½ tsp freshly ground black pepper

1 tsp saffron threads

¼ cup white wine

1 (28oz) can diced tomatoes

4 cups seafood stock

1 bay leaf

1 dozen little neck clams, scrubbed

8 oz raw large shrimp, peeled and deveined

¾ lb halibut, cut into chunks

Crusty whole-grain bread, for serving

**1.** In a large (5½- to 7¼-quart) Dutch oven, heat the olive oil over medium heat. Add the onion and fennel and sauté for 5 minutes or until they begin to caramelize. Add the garlic. Season with salt, pepper, and saffron and cook for 2 minutes until spices become fragrant.

**2.** Add the wine and cook for 2 minutes, scraping any brown bits from the bottom of the Dutch oven, before adding the tomatoes, seafood stock, and bay leaf. Bring to a boil and then reduce the heat and simmer partially covered for 30 minutes.

**3.** Add clams, cover and cook for 5 minutes. Add shrimp and halibut and cook for 5 minutes more.

**4.** Remove the bay leaf before serving. Garnish with fennel fronds and serve with sliced bread.

**TIP** | Look for seafood stock at your local fish market or grocery store.
Cooking for this length of time only reduces a portion of the alcohol; you can omit the wine or replace with more seafood stock, if desired.

**VARIATION** | Use any kind of seafood for this recipe. Mussels, scallops, and lobster are also awesome—go with whatever looks fresh at the market.

---

**NUTRITION PER SERVING (DOES NOT INCLUDE BREAD)**

Calories **290** • Total Fat **9g** • Saturated Fat **1g** • Cholesterol **210mg** • Sodium **667mg** •
Total Carbohydrate **10g** • Dietary Fiber **3g** • Sugars **4g** • Protein **40g**

# pasta e fagioli

This hearty bean and pasta soup will never be as good as my Italian grandmother's ("Nonni"), but it's close. Filled with vegetables and protein, it's a perfect meal by itself, but a few slices of crusty bread never hurt.

Yield **6 servings**  •  Prep Time **10 minutes**  •  Cook Time **45 minutes**

1 tbsp olive oil

1 onion, chopped

2 carrots, chopped

2 stalks celery, chopped

2 cloves garlic, finely chopped

1 head escarole, chopped

1½ tsp kosher salt

¾ tsp freshly ground black pepper

2 tsp dried basil

2 qt homemade or low-sodium chicken stock

2 (15oz) cans cannellini beans, drained and rinsed

½ cup dry ditalini pasta

Red pepper flakes, to serve

Parmesan cheese, to serve

**1.** In a large (5½- to 7¼-quart) Dutch oven, heat the olive oil over medium heat. Add the onion and sauté for 5 minutes. Add the carrots, celery, and garlic and sauté for 3 minutes more. Add the escarole, salt, pepper, and basil, and cook until the escarole is slightly wilted, 2 to 3 minutes.

**2.** Add the chicken stock and beans. Bring the mixture to a boil, reduce the heat, and simmer for 20 minutes.

**3.** Stir in the pasta and cook for 8 to 10 minutes or until the pasta is tender. Ladle into bowls and serve topped with red pepper flakes and Parmesan cheese.

**4.** Leftovers can be stored in an airtight container in the refrigerator for 3 to 4 days or in the freezer for up to 3 months.

**TIP** | If you can't find escarole, use kale or Swiss chard.

---

**NUTRITION PER SERVING**

Calories **259**  •  Total Fat **5g**  •  Saturated Fat **1g**  •  Cholesterol **0mg**  •  Sodium **669mg**  •  Total Carbohydrate **38g**  •  Dietary Fiber **7g**  •  Sugars **4g**  •  Protein **15g**

# **barley** stew

A thick and hearty vegetarian stew that will satisfy even the most skeptical vegetable eater. Despite its low calorie count, you will feel full for hours thanks to 11 grams of fiber per serving.

Yield **4 servings** • Prep Time **10 minutes** • Cook Time **35 minutes**

1 tbsp olive oil

1 small onion, diced

2 cloves garlic, chopped

2 tsp chopped fresh thyme

1 tsp kosher salt

½ tsp red pepper flakes

1 cup dry pearled barley

1 qt homemade or low-sodium vegetable stock

1 (14oz) can diced tomatoes

1 medium zucchini, diced

3 cups chopped kale

Parmesan cheese, grated, to serve

1. In a 4½-quart Dutch oven, heat the olive oil over medium-high heat. Add the onion and sauté for 5 minutes. Add the garlic and thyme; season with salt and red pepper flakes. Add the barley and toss to coat with the oil and seasonings.

2. Add the vegetable stock and tomatoes. Bring to a boil, reduce heat, partially cover, and simmer for 20 minutes.

3. Add the zucchini and kale and simmer for 10 minutes more or until barley is tender. Serve topped with grated Parmesan cheese.

4. Leftovers can be refrigerated for 3 to 4 days or stored in the freezer for up to 3 months.

---

**NUTRITION PER SERVING**

Calories **323** • Total fat **9.5g** • Saturated Fat **4.7g** • Cholesterol **10mg** • Sodium **454mg** •

Total Carbohydrate **54g** • Dietary Fiber **11g** • Sugars **6g** • Protein **13g**

# **crispy tofu** with peanut butter noodles

This recipe is a game changer for those who think they don't like tofu. Lightly panfried to crispy golden perfection, it's paired with cucumber and carrot and tossed in a tangy peanut sauce featuring healthy fats.

Yield **6 servings** • Prep Time **15 minutes** • Cook Time **30 minutes**

1 (14oz) container extra-firm tofu

1 lb brown rice spaghetti or rotini

2 tbsp cornstarch

¼ cup canola oil

4 tbsp peanut butter

2 tbsp reduced-sodium soy sauce

1 tbsp rice vinegar

1 tsp sesame oil

1 tsp minced garlic

2 cups grated carrots

2 cups sliced cucumber

Sriracha (optional), to serve

Lime wedges, to garnish

**1.** Drain the tofu and cut into cubes. Gently press with paper towel to remove as much liquid as possible without breaking the pieces.

**2.** In a large (5½- to 7¼-quart) Dutch oven, cook the brown rice pasta according to the package directions. Reserve ¼ cup of the cooking liquid, drain, and set aside. Wipe out the Dutch oven.

**3.** In a medium bowl, toss the cubed tofu with cornstarch. Return the Dutch oven to the stove top, add the canola oil, and heat over medium heat. Once hot, add the tofu and cook, turning frequently, for 10 to 12 minutes or until the tofu is crispy and golden on all sides. (This may need to be done in batches to avoid overcrowding the pan.)

**4.** While the tofu is cooking, prepare the peanut sauce. In a small bowl, whisk together the peanut butter, soy sauce, vinegar, sesame oil, garlic, and reserved pasta water. Continue to whisk until sauce is completely smooth.

**5.** Pour the sauce over the cooked pasta and toss well to coat. Serve the pasta with the crispy tofu, grated carrots, and sliced cucumber. Top with Sriracha, if desired, and a wedge of lime.

**TIP** | For extra crispy tofu, dice and drain overnight in the refrigerator.

**NUTRITION PER SERVING**

Calories **496** • Total Fat **32g** • Saturated Fat **4g** • Cholesterol **0mg** • Sodium **376mg** •
Total Carbohydrate **25g** • Dietary Fiber **6g** • Sugars **1g** • Protein **34g**

# lightened-up **bolognese**

This hearty pasta dish is made up of a few simple ingredients, all balanced to make each other shine. With lots of vegetables, lean meat, and pasta, this is the essential one-pot dinner. Make the sauce ahead and freeze.

Yield **6 servings** • Prep Time **5 minutes** • Cook Time **25 minutes**

---

1 lb flat, wide pasta, such as pappardelle or broken lasagna noodles

1 tbsp olive oil

2 oz pancetta, finely chopped

½ cup chopped onion

½ cup chopped carrots

½ cup chopped celery

2 cloves garlic, chopped

1 tsp kosher salt

½ tsp freshly ground black pepper

1 tsp dried oregano

1 lb 90% lean ground beef

½ (28oz) can crushed tomatoes

**1.** Cook pasta in a large (5½- to 7¼-quart) Dutch oven according to package directions. Reserve 1 cup of the cooking liquid, then drain, and set cooked pasta and reserved water aside.

**2.** Return the Dutch oven to the stove and heat the olive oil over medium-high heat. Add the pancetta and cook for 3 to 5 minutes until crispy.

**3.** Add the onion, carrots, celery, and garlic to the pot. Season with salt, pepper, and oregano and cook for 5 minutes, until vegetables begin to soften.

**4.** Add the beef and cook, breaking it up with a spoon until browned, then add tomatoes. Bring to a simmer and cook for 10 minutes (or longer if desired). Add pasta and ½ of the pasta water; toss to coat in the sauce. Add more pasta water if needed and cook for an additional 1 to 2 minutes. Serve hot.

**5.** Store leftovers in an airtight container in the refrigerator for up to 4 days. Sauce can be stored in the freezer for up to 3 months.

**TIP** | For some extra heat, serve with a big pinch of red pepper flakes.

**VARIATION** | For a vegan version, omit the pancetta and replace the ground beef with crumbled tempeh.

---

**NUTRITION PER SERVING**

94   Calories **514** • Total Fat **16g** • Saturated Fat **5.5g** • Cholesterol **75mg** • Sodium **530mg** •
Total Carbohydrate **62g** • Dietary Fiber **4g** • Sugars **3g** • Protein **34g**

# **mussels** with white wine

An ideal summer meal when served with a big salad and a loaf of crusty bread to dip in the steamy broth. Mussels are chockful of energy-producing vitamin B12 as well as minerals like iron and the antioxidant selenium.

Yield **4 servings** • Prep Time **10 minutes** • Cook Time **4 minutes**

1 tbsp olive oil

1 tbsp unsalted butter

2 cloves garlic, chopped

Juice and zest of 1 lemon

1 tsp kosher salt

½ tsp freshly ground black pepper

¾ cup dry white wine (Sancerre or sauvignon blanc recommended)

2 lb fresh mussels, scrubbed and rinsed

⅓ cup chopped fresh parsley

Crusty bread (optional), to serve

**1.** In a large (5½- to 7¼-quart) Dutch oven, heat the olive oil and butter over medium-high heat. Once hot, add the garlic and sauté for 1 minute. Add the lemon juice and zest, salt, pepper, and white wine.

**2.** Increase the heat to high and bring to a simmer. Once simmering, add the mussels and toss well. Reduce the heat to medium, cover the pot, and cook for 3 minutes. Remove lid and check to make sure all the shells have opened. (Discard any unopened mussels.)

**3.** Sprinkle with fresh parsley and serve immediately with crusty bread, if desired.

**NUTRITION PER SERVING (DOES NOT INCLUDE BREAD)**

Calories **189** • Total Fat **9g** • Saturated Fat **3g** • Cholesterol **39mg** • Sodium **624mg** •

Total Carbohydrate **5g** • Dietary Fiber **0g** • Sugars **0g** • Protein **14g**

# **chili** with cornbread topping

When made with lean meat and tons of vegetables, chili can be a tremendously healthy meal. This recipe takes it to the next level with a crusty topping made with whole-grain cornmeal.

Yield **6 servings**  •  Prep Time **15 minutes**  •  Cook Time **50 minutes**

1 lb 90% lean ground beef

1 small yellow onion, diced

2 cloves garlic, chopped

1 green bell pepper, roughly chopped

1 tsp kosher salt

1½ tsp ground cumin

2 tsp chili powder

2 (28oz) cans diced tomatoes

1 (15oz) can kidney beans, drained and rinsed

Scallions, chopped (optional), to garnish

**For the topping**
1 cup cornmeal

½ cup all-purpose flour

¼ cup granulated sugar

2 tsp baking powder

¾ tsp kosher salt

1 egg

¾ cup whole milk

2 tbsp unsalted butter, melted

1. Preheat the oven to 375°F. Heat a 4½-quart Dutch oven over medium heat. Once hot, add the ground beef and sauté until browned. Add the onion, garlic, and pepper, and season with salt, cumin, and chili powder. Sauté for 5 minutes. Add the tomatoes and beans and simmer for 10 minutes.

2. Meanwhile, make the topping. In a medium bowl, mix the cornmeal, flour, sugar, baking powder, and salt. Add the egg, milk, and melted butter and stir until well combined.

3. Remove the chili from the heat and pour the cornmeal batter over the top. Transfer to the oven and bake for 25 minutes or until golden brown. Serve warm with chopped scallions to garnish, if desired.

4. Store leftovers in an airtight container in the refrigerator for up to 4 days.

**TIP** | This chili is delicious without the topping as well. Just prepare recipe to step 3 and simmer on the stove top for 30 minutes.

**VARIATION** | This recipe can also be made in a larger Dutch oven, but because the cornbread topping will be spread more thinly, adjust the baking time to 20 minutes.

**NUTRITION PER SERVING**
Calories **435**  •  Total Fat **14g**  •  Saturated Fat **6g**  •  Cholesterol **95mg**  •  Sodium **674mg**  •
Total Carbohydrate **53g**  •  Dietary Fiber **8g**  •  Sugars **16g**  •  Protein **26g**

# asparagus + turkey bacon
## frittata

Egg dishes for dinner have the perfect balance of casual and elegant. This high-protein, low-carb dish is ready in minutes and is ultra satisfying. Save the leftovers for tomorrow's breakfast.

Yield **4 servings** • Prep Time **10 minutes** • Cook Time **15 minutes**

2 tsp olive oil

1 small bunch asparagus, trimmed and chopped

¾ tsp kosher salt

½ tsp freshly ground black pepper

8 eggs, beaten

4 strips cooked turkey bacon, chopped

1 cup shredded Gruyere cheese

**1.** In a large (5½- to 7¼-quart) Dutch oven, heat the olive oil over medium-high heat. Add the asparagus and sauté for 3 to 5 minutes. Season with salt and pepper. Preheat the broiler to high.

**2.** Add the eggs and turkey bacon to the pan and gently stir. Cook for 3 to 4 minutes more, until eggs begin to set.

**3.** Sprinkle with cheese and transfer to broiler. Broil for 2 to 3 minutes or until cheese is melted and slightly golden.

**4.** Use a spatula to remove the frittata from the Dutch oven, and transfer it to a plate or cutting board to slice. Serve warm or at room temperature.

**5.** Store leftovers in an airtight container in the refrigerator for up to 3 days or in the freezer for 1 month.

---

**NUTRITION PER SERVING**

Calories **318** • Total Fat **22g** • Saturated Fat **8g** • Cholesterol **365mg** • Sodium **643mg** • Total Carbohydrate **3g** • Dietary Fiber **1g** • Sugars **2g** • Protein **25g**

# root veggie pasta

A stellar vegetarian recipe that is colorful, savory, and satisfying. This pasta dish highlights high-fiber root vegetables that are typically lost in the background of a recipe. I think you will agree they deserve the spotlight.

Yield **6 servings** • Prep Time **10 minutes** • Cook Time **20 minutes**

1 (15oz) can cannellini beans

1 lb penne

3 tbsp olive oil

½ red onion, thinly sliced

1 bulb fennel, thinly sliced

2 large carrots, thinly sliced

4 cloves garlic, chopped

1 tbsp chopped fresh thyme leaves

½ cup grated Parmesan cheese

1 cup fresh basil, roughly chopped

**1.** Drain and rinse beans and leave them in the colander.

**2.** In a large (5½- to 7¼-quart) Dutch oven, cook the pasta according to package directions in salted water. Reserve 1 cup of the cooking liquid and then drain the pasta by pouring in the same colander as the beans. (This will heat the beans.)

**3.** Return the Dutch oven to the stove over medium-high heat. Add the olive oil, followed by the onion, fennel, carrot, garlic, and thyme, and sauté 5 to 7 minutes until tender.

**4.** Add the cooked pasta, beans, reserved cooking liquid, Parmesan cheese, and basil. Toss gently and serve immediately.

**5.** Store leftovers in an airtight container in the refrigerator for up to 4 days or in the freezer for up to 3 months.

**TIP** | Like a little kick? Sprinkle with a generous dose of red pepper flakes.

**NUTRITION PER SERVING**

Calories **461** • Total Fat **12g** • Saturated Fat **3g** • Cholesterol **10mg** • Sodium **210mg** •

Total Carbohydrate **73g** • Dietary Fiber **8g** • Sugars **5g** • Protein **19g**

# turkey tater tot bake

This kid-friendly meal is packed with lean protein, veggies, and tons of flavor. Sweet potato tots are an easy and fun topping for a hearty mix of seasoned lean ground turkey, onion, and bell pepper.

Yield **6 servings**  •  Prep Time **10 minutes**  •  Cook Time **40 minutes**

1 tbsp canola oil

1 lb 93% lean ground turkey

2 cloves garlic, minced

1 onion, chopped

1 red bell pepper, chopped

1 tsp kosher salt

1 tsp dried oregano

1 tbsp all-purpose flour

½ cup low-sodium chicken or vegetable broth

1 (20oz) package frozen sweet potato tots (Alexia brand recommended)

1 cup crumbled feta cheese

Fresh chives, chopped, to garnish

**1.** Preheat the oven to 425°F. In a large (5½- to 7¼-quart) Dutch oven, heat the canola oil over medium heat. Once hot, add the ground turkey and sauté for 5 minutes to brown, breaking up the meat with a spatula or wooden spoon. Add the garlic, onion, and pepper. Stir and season with salt, and oregano.

**2.** Sprinkle with flour, stir, and cook for 2 to 3 minutes. Pour in the chicken broth and stir.

**3.** Place the sweet potato tots on top of the turkey mixture. Transfer to the oven and bake for 25 minutes. Top with feta and return to the oven to broil for an additional 3 to 4 minutes.

**4.** Remove from the oven and sprinkle with chives before serving. To freeze, allow to cool completely, cover, and freeze for up to 3 months.

**TIP** | To make gluten-free, omit the flour and add 2 teaspoons cornstarch to chicken broth; stir together before adding to the pot.

---

**NUTRITION PER SERVING**

Calories **457**  •  Total Fat **22g**  •  Saturated Fat **8g**  •  Cholesterol **164mg**  •  Sodium **683mg**  •  Total Carbohydrate **17g**  •  Dietary Fiber **3g**  •  Sugars **9g**  •  Protein **41g**

# tuna noodle bake

Creamy and comforting, this baked pasta dish requires minimal prep work and is ready in under 30 minutes. Tuna is an excellent source of the oh-so-powerful omega-3 fats, which are vital for healthy skin, circulation, and brain health.

Yield **6 servings**  •  Prep Time **10 minutes**  •  Cook Time **30 minutes**

12 oz uncooked egg noodles

½ cup panko bread crumbs

1 tbsp olive oil

3 tbsp unsalted butter

3 tbsp all-purpose flour

2 cups chicken broth

1 cup whole milk

1 tsp kosher salt

⅛ tsp ground nutmeg

½ tsp dried thyme

2 (5oz) cans tuna, drained

1 cup frozen peas

2 cups sliced mushrooms

**1.** In a large (5½- to 7¼-quart) Dutch oven, bring 6 cups of salted water to a boil. Add the pasta and cook for 6 minutes. Drain and set aside.

**2.** Preheat the oven to 375°F. In a small bowl, mix the bread crumbs and olive oil. Set aside.

**3.** Wipe out the Dutch oven and return to the stove top. Add the butter and melt over medium heat. Once the butter has melted, sprinkle with flour and stir with a wooden spoon for 2 to 3 minutes.

**4.** Whisk in the chicken broth and increase the heat to bring to a boil, stirring constantly. Once thickened, whisk in the milk. Stir in the salt, nutmeg, and thyme. Mix in the noodles, followed by the tuna, peas, and mushrooms. Mix well to combine.

**5.** Sprinkle the bread crumb mixture over the top. Bake for 20 minutes, uncovered, until heated through and topping is golden brown.

**VARIATION**  |  Instead of mushrooms, try tomatoes and spinach.

**NUTRITION PER SERVING**

Calories **458**  •  Total Fat **17g**  •  Saturated Fat **6g**  •  Cholesterol **80mg**  •  Sodium **652mg**  •

Total Carbohydrate **50g**  •  Dietary Fiber **4g**  •  Sugars **4g**  •  Protein **25g**

# baking dish

# **eggplant** stackers

This tender roasted eggplant is filled with sauce, basil, and cheese. Move over eggplant Parmesan, there's a lighter and healthier casserole for you to crave.

Yield **6 servings** • Prep time **10 minutes** • Cook time **40 minutes**

2 medium eggplant (see tip)

3 tbsp olive oil

1½ tsp kosher salt

Freshly ground black pepper to taste

1½ cups marinara sauce (see variation)

8 oz fresh mozzarella, cut into 6 slices

24 fresh basil leaves

½ cup panko bread crumbs

**1.** Preheat the oven to 400°F.

**2.** Slice each eggplant into 6 rounds, each ¼- to ½-inch thick. Arrange 6 eggplant rounds on the bottom of a 9 x 13-inch baking dish. Drizzle with 1½ tablespoons olive oil and season with ¾ teaspoon salt and black pepper. Stack the remaining 6 eggplant rounds on top and season with the remaining olive oil, salt, and pepper. Bake for 15 minutes, turn over each stack, and bake for 15 minutes more. Remove from the oven.

**3.** Remove the top layer of eggplant from each stack. On each bottom layer, place 2 tablespoons marinara sauce, 1 slice mozzarella, and 4 basil leaves. Replace the top layer of eggplant. Drizzle the remaining sauce over top and sprinkle with panko bread crumbs.

**4.** Bake for 10 minutes more, or until cheese is melted and panko is crispy. Remove from the oven and allow to cool for 5 to 10 minutes before serving.

**5.** To freeze, cool to room temperature and transfer to an airtight container. Freeze for up to 3 months.

**TIP** | Eggplant can vary greatly in size and circumference. If you have long, thin eggplant, you may be able to create up to 12 smaller stacks in your baking dish. Make as many stacks as possible and divide the filling ingredients evenly among them.

**VARIATION** | To make your own marinara sauce, sauté ½ cup chopped onion, 2 cloves minced garlic, and ½ teaspoon ground fennel in 2 tablespoons olive oil. Add 1 (28oz) can crushed tomatoes, season with salt and pepper, and simmer for at least 20 minutes, stirring occasionally.

---

**NUTRITION PER SERVING**

Calories **263** • Total fat **16g** • Saturated Fat **6g** • Cholesterol **41mg** • Sodium **439mg** •

Total Carbohydrate **17g** • Dietary Fiber **6g** • Sugars **9g** • Protein **10g**

# grilled cheese sandwich
## casserole

This is simply the best way to make sandwiches for a crowd; you can mix up the fillings with everyone's favorites. It's also a great way to add more vegetables to a meal—stuff those sammies with any and all veggies!

Yield **12 sandwiches** • Prep time **5 minutes** • Cook time **15 minutes**

1 pkg potato bread dinner rolls (12 rolls; see tip)

12 slices deli cheese, such as cheddar, Swiss, or American

1 tbsp olive oil

1 clove garlic, minced

¼ tsp kosher salt

Freshly ground black pepper

**Optional toppings**

Turkey and baby spinach

Tomato and bacon

Ham and Granny Smith apple slices

**1.** Preheat the oven to 350°F. Line a 9 x 13-inch baking dish with aluminum foil, leaving extra foil to hang off either side of the dish. (This will help you lift the sandwiches out of the pan after baking.)

**2.** Without separating the rolls, slice lengthwise and place the bottom piece in the prepared baking dish. Top the bread with cheese slices, followed by desired toppings. Place top piece of bread over the fillings.

**3.** In a small bowl, combine the olive oil, garlic, salt, and pepper to taste. Brush this mixture over the top of the bread. Bake for 12 to 15 minutes or until cheese is melted and top of bread is golden brown. Remove from the oven, cut, and serve. Leftovers can be reheated in a 350°F oven until warm.

**TIP** | Look for small rolls that are joined together at the edges, forming a rectangle.

---

**NUTRITION PER SANDWICH (CHEESE ONLY)**

Calories **215** • Total Fat **9g** • Saturated Fat **5g** • Cholesterol **25mg** • Sodium **396mg** • Total Carbohydrate **20g** • Dietary Fiber **1g** • Sugars **4g** • Protein **12g**

# sausage + quinoa
## stuffed peppers

This gluten-free, high-protein, veggie-filled recipe puts everything you want from a meal into a pretty little pepper package. Experiment with various fillings and find your family's favorite combo.

Yield **6 servings**  •  Prep time **15 minutes**  •  Cook time **55 minutes**     GF

6 red bell peppers

1 tbsp olive oil, divided

8 oz chicken sausage, diced (Aidells brand recommended)

2 cups diced, peeled eggplant

1 cup sliced mushrooms

¼ cup finely chopped red onion

½ tsp kosher salt

¼ tsp black pepper

1 cup cannellini beans, rinsed and drained

1 clove garlic, minced

2 tsp chopped fresh thyme

½ cup low-sodium chicken broth, divided

1 cup marinara sauce

1½ cups cooked quinoa

½ cup shredded mozzarella cheese

1. Preheat the oven to 350°F. Lay the peppers on their sides and thinly slice a piece off the bottom to create a flat surface. Cut off tops of peppers and scoop out seeds, set aside.

2. In a skillet, heat 1 teaspoon olive oil over medium-high heat. Add the sausage and cook for 4 to 5 minutes until browned. Transfer to a bowl and set aside.

3. Return the skillet to the stove top and heat the remaining olive oil over medium-high heat. Add the eggplant, mushrooms, and onion. Season with salt and pepper and sauté for 5 minutes until tender.

4. Add the beans, garlic, thyme, ¼ cup broth, marinara sauce, and cooked sausage. Continue to cook for an additional 2 minutes and then remove from heat and mix in cooked quinoa.

5. Fill each pepper with the quinoa mixture and top with shredded cheese. Transfer to a 9 x 13-inch baking dish and pour the remaining ¼ cup broth in the bottom of the dish. Cover with foil and bake for 25 minutes; then remove foil and bake for 10 minutes more until peppers are soft and cheese is melted.

**VARIATION** | Make it vegetarian by omitting the sausage and adding extra beans.

**NUTRITION PER SERVING**

Calories **298**  •  Total Fat **10g**  •  Saturated Fat **3g**  •  Cholesterol **35mg**  •  Sodium **659mg**  •

Total Carbohydrate **33g**  •  Dietary Fiber **8g**  •  Sugars **3g**  •  Protein **19g**

# **chicken** enchiladas

Enchiladas are a sensational way to use up leftover chicken or to dress up a store-bought rotisserie chicken. Serve this full-flavor and high-protein dish with a green salad for a spectacular, yet easy to prepare meal.

Yield **4 servings**  •  Prep time **10 minutes**  •  Cook time **15 minutes**       30  FF

1 (2lb) rotisserie chicken

½ tsp ground cumin

½ red bell pepper, finely chopped

3 scallions, chopped (white and green parts)

1 cup salsa verde, divided

1 cup shredded cheddar cheese, divided

8 (6-in) tortillas (corn or flour)

Red onion, chopped (optional), to garnish

Cilantro, chopped (optional), to garnish

**1.** Preheat the oven to 375°F. Spray a 9 x 13-inch baking dish with nonstick cooking spray.

**2.** Remove and discard the skin from the rotisserie chicken. Remove the meat from the bones and transfer to a bowl. (You should have about 3½ cups of meat). Discard the bones and carcass or reserve for stock.

**3.** Add the cumin, bell pepper, and green onion to the bowl, followed by ½ cup salsa and ½ cup shredded cheese. Mix well.

**4.** Scoop ⅛ of the chicken mixture onto the center of a tortilla, roll up, and place in the prepared baking dish. Repeat with the remaining tortillas

**5.** Spread the remaining ½ cup salsa over the tortillas and sprinkle with the remaining ½ cup shredded cheese. Bake for 15 minutes or until cheese is melted and bubbly.

**6.** To freeze, allow to cool completely and cover with a layer of parchment paper and a second layer of aluminum foil. To reheat, go right from freezer to oven; bake at 375°F, covered, for 45 minutes. Remove foil and bake for an additional 15 minutes until cheese is melted. Garnish with chopped red onion and cilantro before serving, if desired.

**TIP** | For easy clean up or freezer meals, prepare this in a disposable tray. This recipe can also be made ahead; refrigerate or freeze before baking.

**VARIATION** | Make a vegetarian version using beans and seasonal vegetables in place of the chicken.

**NUTRITION PER SERVING**

Calories **503**  •  Total Fat **18g**  •  Saturated Fat **8g**  •  Cholesterol **151mg**  •  Sodium **678mg**  •  Total Carbohydrate **33g**  •  Dietary Fiber **2g**  •  Sugars **4g**  •  Protein **51g**

# veggie **lasagna**

Lasagna is often a high-fat dish, but it doesn't have to be. This Italian staple gets a makeover with lower-fat cheese and layers of cooked vegetables, resulting in a delicious dish that has significantly less fat than a traditional lasagna.

Yield **10 servings** • Prep time **20 minutes** • Cook time **1 hour**

3 cups shredded part-skim mozzarella

½ cup grated Parmesan cheese

2 cups part-skim ricotta cheese

2 large eggs, lightly beaten

1 tsp kosher salt

½ tsp freshly ground black pepper

2½ cups marinara sauce

1 (8oz) pkg no-boil lasagna noodles

4 cups cooked vegetables (see tip)

1. Preheat the oven to 375°F. In a small bowl, combine the mozzarella and Parmesan. In another bowl, mix together the ricotta, eggs, salt, and pepper.

2. Pour ½ cup marinara sauce in the bottom of a 9 x 13-inch baking dish and top with a single layer of lasagna noodles. (You may need to break some to fit.)

3. Top with ½ of the vegetables, ⅓ of the marinara sauce, ½ of the ricotta mixture, and ⅓ of the mozzarella mixture.

4. Make the next layer with more noodles, the remaining vegetables, more sauce, and the remaining ricotta, and more cheese. Top with a final layer of noodles, followed by the remaining sauce and cheese.

5. Cover with foil and bake for 40 minutes. Remove the foil and bake for 15 to 20 minutes more, until the cheese is melted and the sauce is bubbling at the edges. Allow to cool for at least 15 minutes before serving.

6. To freeze, allow to cool completely. Wrap tightly in foil or plastic wrap and freeze for up to 3 months.

**TIP** | Sauté or roast vegetables like mushrooms, zucchini, eggplant, onion, and butternut squash. To roast, toss on a sheet pan with olive oil, salt, and pepper and cook at 400°F until tender.

**NUTRITION PER SERVING**

Calories **496** • Total Fat **14g** • Saturated Fat **6g** • Cholesterol **95mg** • Sodium **776mg** • Total Carbohydrate **68g** • Dietary Fiber **10g** • Sugars **8g** • Protein **24g**

# mexican quinoa casserole
## with guacamole

Quinoa is a high-protein superfood that is much more versatile than you might think. This flavorful casserole makes a satisfying vegetarian meal on its own, or it can be served as a side dish with steak or fish.

Yield **4 servings** • Prep time **5 minutes** • Cook time **30 minutes**

3 cups cooked quinoa

1 cup canned black beans, rinsed and drained

½ cup low-sodium vegetable or chicken broth

⅓ cup salsa

⅓ cup shredded cheddar cheese

4 oz whole-grain tortilla chips, to serve

Pickled jalapeños, to serve

**For the guacamole**
2 avocados

Juice of 1 lime

½ tsp kosher salt

Hot sauce, to taste

**1.** Preheat the oven to 375°F. Spray a 9 x 9-inch baking dish with nonstick cooking spray.

**2.** In a medium bowl, combine the quinoa, black beans, vegetable broth, salsa, and cheese. Stir to combine. Pour into the prepared baking dish and bake for 20 minutes.

**3.** Meanwhile, to make the guacamole, peel and dice the avocados. Place in a bowl and mash with the lime juice, salt, and a dash of hot sauce. Taste and add more salt or hot sauce if needed.

**4.** Top the casserole with guacamole and pickled jalapenos and serve with tortilla chips. Store leftovers in an airtight container in the refrigerator for up to 4 days.

**TIP** | Make a large batch of quinoa on the weekend and set some aside to make this dish quickly on a weeknight.

**NUTRITION PER SERVING**
Calories **399** • Total Fat **18g** • Saturated Fat **4g** • Cholesterol **10mg** • Sodium **533mg** •
Total Carbohydrate **46g** • Dietary Fiber **13g** • Sugars **0.5g** • Protein **14g**

# **buffalo cauliflower** casserole

Ditch the greasy chicken wings and make this dish for game day. Low-calorie cauliflower absorbs all the tangy sauce and crisps up without being drenched in oil. Serve in a rice bowl, in a burrito, or on top of a salad.

Yield **6 servings**  •  Prep time **10 minutes**  •  Cook time **30 minutes**

2 heads cauliflower, trimmed and florets separated

½ tsp kosher salt

⅓ cup hot sauce

2 tbsp canola oil

1 cup shredded Mexican cheese blend

½ cup crumbled feta cheese

¼ cup chopped chives, to garnish

**1.** Preheat the oven to 425°F. Spread cauliflower florets in a 9 x 13-inch baking dish and season with salt.

**2.** In a small bowl, whisk hot sauce, canola oil, and 3 tablespoons water. Pour over the cauliflower and toss to coat. Place in the oven and roast for 40 minutes, turning halfway through.

**3.** Sprinkle with the Mexican cheese blend and feta and place under the broiler until the cheese is melted and the edges of the cauliflower are crispy. Top with chives and serve.

---

**NUTRITION PER SERVING**

Calories **229**  •  Total Fat **18g**  •  Saturated Fat **5g**  •  Cholesterol **35mg**  •  Sodium **540mg**  •  Total Carbohydrate **7g**  •  Dietary Fiber **3g**  •  Sugars **3g**  •  Protein **9g**

# sausage + pepper bake with creamy cilantro-mustard sauce

Planning ahead? This simple meal can be prepped and refrigerated for days in advance. Broccoli may seem like an odd addition, but its nutty roasted goodness is the perfect topping along with a tangy, yogurt-based sauce.

Yield **8 servings** • Prep time **10 minutes** • Cook time **25 minutes**

1 red onion, sliced

1 bell pepper, sliced

2 cups chopped broccoli

8 pork sausage links

8 whole-grain hot dog rolls, to serve

**For the sauce**

¼ cup nonfat Greek yogurt

2 tbsp Dijon mustard

2 tsp honey

1 cup chopped fresh cilantro

**1.** To make the sauce, in a blender, combine the yogurt, mustard, honey, cilantro, and ½ cup water. Blend until smooth. Pour into a bowl and set aside.

**2.** Preheat the oven to 425°F. Spread the onion, pepper, and broccoli in a 9 x 13-inch baking dish. Place the sausages on top.

**3.** Bake for 25 minutes until the sausage is cooked through and the vegetables are tender.

**4.** Serve the sausages in rolls, topped with vegetables and mustard sauce.

**NUTRITION PER SERVING**

Calories **344** • Total Fat **17g** • Saturated Fat **5g** • Cholesterol **45mg** • Sodium **485mg** • Total Carbohydrate **28g** • Dietary Fiber **2g** • Sugars **8g** • Protein **20g**

# stuffed **spaghetti squash**

Spaghetti squash is the guilt-free solution to piles of pasta. In this dish, it's jam-packed with protein and spinach and sealed with melted cheese. Roast the squash ahead on a meal-prep day. If you are a fan of chicken Parmesan, add a few spoonfuls of marinara sauce before baking.

Yield **2 servings** • Prep time **10 minutes** • Cook time **50 minutes**

1 medium spaghetti squash, halved lengthwise and seeds removed

1 tbsp olive oil

1 tsp salt

3 cups cooked diced chicken or sliced chicken sausage

2 cups baby spinach

1 cup shredded part-skim mozzarella

1 tsp dried Italian seasoning

**1.** Preheat the oven to 400°F. Place the squash in a 9 x 13-inch baking dish, drizzle with olive oil, and season with salt. Turn the squash cut-side down and roast for 40 minutes.

**2.** Remove the squash from the oven, turn, and fill each half with chicken (or chicken sausage) and spinach. Top with cheese and Italian seasoning.

**3.** Return to the oven and bake until the cheese is melted and the filling is heated through, about 10 minutes more. Broil for last 2 minutes of cooking to make the cheese extra bubbly.

**NUTRITION PER SERVING**

Calories **445** • Total Fat **10g** • Saturated Fat **3g** • Cholesterol **171mg** • Sodium **329mg** •

Total Carbohydrate **21g** • Dietary Fiber **5g** • Sugars **8g** • Protein **38g**

# turkey + stuffing roll-ups

Why wait for Thanksgiving to have turkey? This fresh take on the holiday staples of turkey, stuffing, and cranberry sauce can be thrown together on any weeknight. Leftovers are day-after-Thanksgiving caliber!

Yield **4 servings** • Prep time **15 minutes** • Cook time **30 minutes**

8 (2oz) turkey cutlets

4 cups cubed whole-grain, day-old bread (see tip)

1 cup chicken stock

½ tsp kosher salt

½ tsp poultry seasoning

1 tsp Dijon mustard

2 cloves garlic, minced

½ apple, finely chopped

**For the cranberry sauce**

2 cups fresh or frozen cranberries

2 tbsp honey

Juice and zest ½ orange

Pinch salt

1. Preheat the oven to 400°F. Working in batches, place the turkey cutlets in a resealable plastic bag and pound to flatten; set aside.

2. In a medium bowl, combine the cubed bread, chicken stock, salt, poultry seasoning, mustard, garlic, and apple. Mix well to combine. (Clean hands work best for this!)

3. Lay the cutlets flat and place about 2 tablespoons of stuffing in the middle of each. Roll up and place in a 9 x 13-inch baking dish. Cover with aluminum foil and bake for 25 minutes. After 25 minutes, remove the foil and bake for 5 minutes more.

4. While the turkey is in the oven, make the cranberry sauce. Combine the cranberries, honey, orange juice and zest, and a pinch of salt in a microwave-safe bowl. Microwave for 2 minutes. Stir and microwave for 1 minute more. The sauce will thicken as it cools.

5. Serve hot with cranberry sauce spooned over the top or on the side for dipping.

**TIP** | Don't have day-old bread? Toast fresh bread cubes in the oven to dry them out.

---

**NUTRITION PER SERVING**

Calories **498** • Total Fat **7g** • Saturated Fat **2g** • Cholesterol **206mg** • Sodium **534mg** •
Total Carbohydrate **38g** • Dietary Fiber **6g** • Sugars **16g** • Protein **43g**

# fennel + white bean gratin

This dish, a green salad with a lemony vinaigrette, and a glass of white wine may be all you need in life. Fennel is a natural digestive aid, and it holds up to the high heat of the oven when baked in a delicate ricotta custard. If you mix leftovers with pasta, no one will judge you.

Yield **4 servings**  •  Prep time **10 minutes**  •  Cook time **35 minutes**

2 tbsp olive oil

1 large bulb fennel, thinly sliced

3 cloves garlic, chopped

½ tsp kosher salt

½ tsp freshly ground black pepper

8 oz part-skim ricotta cheese

2 oz crème fraîche

1 egg, beaten

⅓ cup grated Parmesan cheese

1 (15oz) can cannellini beans, drained and rinsed

⅓ cup panko bread crumbs

½ cup chopped fresh parsley, to garnish

**1.** Preheat the oven to 425°F. Spray a 9 x 9-inch baking dish with nonstick cooking spray and set aside.

**2.** In a medium skillet, heat 1 tablespoon olive oil over medium-high heat. Add the fennel and garlic, season with salt and pepper, and sauté for 5 minutes to soften and brown slightly.

**3.** In a medium bowl, mix the ricotta, crème fraîche, egg, and Parmesan cheese. Add the fennel mixture and beans to the ricotta and gently stir to combine. Pour the combined mixture into the prepared baking dish.

**4.** In a small bowl, mix the bread crumbs with the remaining 1 tablespoon olive oil and sprinkle over the casserole.

**5.** Cover with foil and place in the oven for 15 minutes. Remove the foil and cook for an additional 15 minutes, or until the edges are bubbling and the topping is golden brown. Sprinkle with parsley and serve.

**NUTRITION PER SERVING**

Calories **339**  •  Total Fat **20g**  •  Saturated Fat **8g**  •  Cholesterol **82mg**  •  Sodium **445mg**  •  Total Carbohydrate **23g**  •  Dietary Fiber **6g**  •  Sugars **1g**  •  Protein **17g**

# ravioli bake

This ravioli hack is a great way to give new life to leftover vegetables. Make trays ahead of time and freeze for an effortless dinner on a busy weeknight. Use homemade marinara, or look for a good quality jarred sauce without a lot of additives, such as Rao's or Newman's Own.

Yield **6 servings**  •  Prep time **5 minutes**  •  Cook time **20 minutes**          V    30    FF

1 (20oz) pkg refrigerated cheese ravioli

2 cups prepared marinara sauce

2 cups cooked vegetables, such as steamed broccoli, roasted butternut squash, sautéed onions

1 cup shredded part-skim mozzarella

**1.** Preheat the oven to 350°F. Spray a 9 x 13-inch baking dish with nonstick cooking spray.

**2.** Place the ravioli, marinara sauce, and vegetables into the prepared dish and mix gently to make sure all ingredients are well dispersed.

**3.** Sprinkle with cheese and bake for 20 minutes or until the cheese is melted and bubbly.

**4.** To freeze for a later time, sprinkle with cheese (do not bake), cover with foil, and store in the freezer for up to 3 months. To reheat, bake covered in a 350°F oven for 25 minutes. Remove the foil, return to the oven, and bake until the cheese is melted and bubbly, about 20 minutes more.

**TIP** | Put the casserole under the broiler for the last minute to make the cheese golden and nutty.

**NUTRITION PER SERVING**

Calories **446**  •  Total Fat **15g**  •  Saturated Fat **6g**  •  Cholesterol **63mg**  •  Sodium **663mg**  •

Total Carbohydrate **60g**  •  Dietary Fiber **11g**  •  Sugars **15g**  •  Protein **22g**

# **no-cook chicken** tabbouleh

This is the ideal homemade recipe for when you just don't feel like cooking. Cubes of juicy mango and fresh mint add a refreshing burst of flavor. Make this hearty salad and dressing ahead of time and toss right before serving.

Yield **4 servings** • Prep time **2 hours** • Cook time **none**

1½ cups bulgur wheat

1½ cups low-sodium chicken broth

8 oz cooked chicken, shredded or diced

1 mango, diced

3 tbsp chopped fresh parsley

3 tbsp chopped fresh mint

1 medium cucumber, chopped

1 cup cherry tomatoes, quartered

**For the dressing**

2 tbsp tahini

Juice of ½ lemon

1 tbsp honey

½ tsp minced garlic

¼ tsp kosher salt

⅛ tsp freshly ground black pepper

1. Place bulgur wheat in a 9 x 9-inch baking dish. Heat the broth in the microwave for 5 minutes or until simmering. Pour the hot broth over the bulgur, stir gently, then cover with plastic wrap and refrigerate for 2 hours.

2. To make the dressing, combine tahini, lemon juice, honey, garlic, and ¼ cup water; season with salt and pepper and set aside.

3. When the bulgur is ready, top with the shredded chicken, mango, parsley, mint, cucumber, and tomatoes. Add tahini dressing and toss to combine.

4. Store leftovers in an airtight container in the refrigerator for up to 4 days.

**NUTRITION PER SERVING**

Calories **399** • Total Fat **8g** • Saturated Fat **2g** • Cholesterol **48mg** • Sodium **203mg** •

Total Carbohydrate **57g** • Dietary Fiber **12g** • Sugars **12g** • Protein **28g**

# **arepa** casserole

Arepas are a scrumptious corn cake popular in Latin cooking. They are typically served stuffed and eaten out of hand, but in this version, a large arepa "crust" is topped pulled pork, tomatoes, and avocado. Adapt this basic recipe with whatever toppings you like, from shrimp to scrambled eggs.

Yield **6 servings** • Prep time **5 minutes** • Cook time **25 minutes**

2 cups masarepa corn meal

2 tsp kosher salt

1 batch Pulled Pork (page 146)

2 avocados, diced

1 cup diced fresh tomatoes

Pickled jalapeños

**1.** Preheat the oven to 450°F. In a medium bowl, combine the masarepa, salt, and 2 cups water. Mix until a soft dough forms.

**2.** Press the dough into an oiled 9 x 13-inch baking dish. Bake for 20 minutes, and then broil for 2 minutes, until the edges are golden brown.

**3.** Remove from the oven and top with pulled pork, avocado, tomato, and pickled jalapeños.

**TIP** | Look for Goya brand masarepa in the Latin foods section of the grocery store. Regular corn meal cannot be substituted.

**VARIATION** | For a vegetarian version, top with grilled vegetables. Add some crumbled Mexican cheese over the top.

**NUTRITION PER SERVING**

122   Calories **522** • Total Fat **17g** • Saturated Fat **3g** • Cholesterol **73mg** • Sodium **840mg** • Total Carbohydrate **53g** • Dietary Fiber **8g** • Sugars **5g** • Protein **36g**

# **summer squash** casserole

A lighter take on famous Southern dish that is hands down the best thing to do with a surplus of squash from the garden. Eggs and Greek yogurt boost the protein and there's plenty of hunger-fighting fiber. Serve this dish on its own or as a side with roasted chicken or grilled fish.

Yield **4 servings**  •  Prep time **15 minutes**  •  Cook time **55 minutes**

3 large eggs

2 tbsp mayonnaise

3 tbsp plain low-fat Greek yogurt

1 tsp kosher salt

½ tsp freshly ground black pepper

2 tbsp chopped fresh oregano or 2 tsp dried oregano

1 cup shredded sharp cheddar cheese

1 zucchini, sliced

2 yellow squash, sliced

1 small onion, cut in half and sliced

¼ cup panko bread crumbs

Fresh basil for serving

**1.** Preheat the oven to 400°F. Coat a 9 x 13-inch baking dish with nonstick cooking spray and set aside.

**2.** In a large bowl, whisk eggs, mayonnaise, Greek yogurt, salt, pepper, and oregano. Fold in the cheese, followed by the zucchini, yellow squash, and onion.

**3.** Transfer the mixture to the prepared baking dish. Cover with foil and bake for 25 minutes.

**4.** Remove the foil, sprinkle with the bread crumbs, return to the oven, and bake uncovered for an additional 30 minutes or until the bread crumbs are golden brown. Top with fresh basil and serve.

**5.** Store in an airtight container and cool completely before refrigerating or freezing.

**NUTRITION PER SERVING**

Calories **329**  •  Total Fat **16g**  •  Saturated Fat **7g**  •  Cholesterol **171mg**  •  Sodium **660mg**  •

Total Carbohydrate **20g**  •  Dietary Fiber **4g**  •  Sugars **11g**  •  Protein **28g**

# mediterranean hasselback
# **sweet potatoes**

This satisfying meal is bursting with flavor and nutrients. The hasselback presentation looks impressive but is easy to execute. Sun-dried tomatoes, olives, and feta cheese balance the earthy sweetness of the potatoes.

Yield **6 servings** • Prep time **10 minutes** • Cook time **60 minutes**

6 medium sweet potatoes

2 tbsp olive oil

1 tsp kosher salt

¼ tsp freshly ground black pepper

**For the topping**

½ cup sliced Kalamata olives

½ cup oil-packed sun-dried tomatoes, drained and chopped

½ cup crumbled feta cheese

1 cup canned chickpeas, roughly chopped

3 scallions, finely chopped

1. Preheat the oven to 425°F and line a 9 x 13-inch baking dish with parchment paper.

2. Using a sharp knife, make a series of ⅛-inch slices along the top of each potato, going only two thirds of the way down so that the potato remains in one piece. Transfer to the prepared baking dish.

3. Drizzle potatoes with olive oil and season with salt and pepper. Bake for 50 to 60 minutes until tender.

4. While potatoes are cooking, prepare the topping. In a medium bowl, combine the olives, sun-dried tomatoes, feta, chickpeas, and scallions. Toss to combine.

5. As soon as the potatoes come out of the oven, spoon the olive and bean mixture over the top, being sure to tuck some of the mixture between the slices of sweet potato.

6. Serve warm or at room temperature. Store leftovers in an airtight container in the refrigerator for 3 to 4 days.

**TIP** | If your sweet potatoes won't sit upright, cut a small piece off the bottom to help them lay flat.

**VARIATION** | Chickpeas give this recipe a plant-based protein boost! You can also make this recipe with cooked chicken or salmon.

**NUTRITION PER SERVING**

Calories **267** • Total Fat **10g** • Saturated Fat **3g** • Cholesterol **11mg** • Sodium **458mg** •

Total Carbohydrate **37g** • Dietary Fiber **7g** • Sugars **7g** • Protein **7g**

# pesto + broccoli stuffed shells

I used to be so intimidated by making stuffed shells, and while they do require a few steps, they couldn't be easier to make. If you share my fear, this is the ideal starter recipe! This casserole-style pasta bake comes complete with a veggie—roasted broccoli—plus plenty of protein from low-fat cheeses.

Yield **6 servings**  •  Prep time **20 minutes**  •  Cook time **40 minutes**

24 large, uncooked pasta shells (make a few extra as some may break when boiling)

12 oz part-skim ricotta cheese

¼ cup grated Parmesan cheese

1 large egg

½ tsp kosher salt

½ tsp freshly ground black pepper

¼ cup prepared pesto sauce

⅓ cup heavy cream

3 cups broccoli florets

1 cup shredded part-skim mozzarella

**1.** Cook shells in boiling salted water according to package directions; drain and set aside.

**2.** Preheat the oven to 400°F. In a medium bowl, mix the ricotta, Parmesan cheese, egg, salt, and pepper. Set aside.

**3.** In a separate microwave-safe bowl, mix the pesto and heavy cream. Microwave for 2 minutes. Set aside.

**4.** Spoon 1 heaping tablespoon of ricotta mixture into each shell and place in a 9 x 13-inch baking dish.

**5.** Add the broccoli to the baking dish, tucking it in corners and between shells. Sprinkle with mozzarella and pour the pesto cream mixture over the top.

**6.** Cover with foil and bake for 35 minutes; remove foil and back for 5 minutes more.

**7.** Allow to cool for 5 minutes before serving. To freeze, cover before baking and store in the freezer for up to 3 months.

**VARIATION** | Not a fan of pesto? Make this recipe with marinara sauce instead.

**NUTRITION PER SERVING**

Calories **501**  •  Total Fat **20g**  •  Saturated Fat **10g**  •  Cholesterol **162mg**  •  Sodium **627mg**  •  Total Carbohydrate **55g**  •  Dietary Fiber **2g**  •  Sugars **1g**  •  Protein **29g**

# chicken + rice casserole

Like the casserole version of chicken soup, this hands-off recipe is pure comfort food. Toss all the ingredients into a dish and bake—there's virtually no active time—and the result is perfectly cooked rice lightly flavored with lemon and savory roasted chicken.

Yield **4 servings**  •  Prep time **5 minutes**  •  Cook time **60 minutes**     GF  DF

1½ cups uncooked white rice

3 cups homemade or low-sodium chicken stock

1 tsp poultry seasoning

1 tsp kosher salt

½ tsp freshly ground black pepper

Zest of 1 lemon

8 chicken drumsticks

**1.** Preheat the oven to 375°F.

**2.** In a 9 x 13-inch baking dish, combine the rice, chicken stock, poultry seasoning, salt, pepper, and lemon zest. Stir well.

**3.** Season the drumsticks with additional salt and pepper and arrange them on the rice. Cover with a piece of parchment paper and a piece of aluminum foil. Place in the oven and bake for 40 minutes.

**4.** Remove the foil and parchment and cook for an additional 20 minutes or until the chicken reaches an internal temperature of 165°F.

**5.** Store leftovers in an airtight container in the refrigerator for up to 4 days.

**TIP** | The cilantro-mustard sauce that accompanies the Sausage + Pepper Bake (page 114) is also excellent with this dish.

**NUTRITION PER SERVING**

Calories **422**  •  Total Fat **6g**  •  Saturated Fat **1.5g**  •  Cholesterol **81mg**  •  Sodium **511mg**  •

Total Carbohydrate **46g**  •  Dietary Fiber **1g**  •  Sugars **0g**  •  Protein **30g**

# multicooker + slow cooker

# coconut **chicken**

A spin on butter chicken, only no butter! Make this a perfectly balanced meal and serve with brown rice or naan bread, which pair nicely with the classic Indian spices in this dish.

Yield **8 servings**  •  Prep time **8 minutes**  •  Cook time **4 to 8 hours**

1 cup all-purpose flour

½ tsp kosher salt

1½ lb boneless, skinless chicken thighs

1 tbsp coconut oil

1 (14oz) can coconut milk

½ cup marinara sauce

1 red onion, sliced

2 garlic cloves, sliced

½ cup chopped pineapple (fresh or canned)

Juice of 1 lime

1 tbsp grated fresh ginger

1 tbsp curry powder

2 tsp ground turmeric

1 tsp celery salt

1 tsp ground cumin

**To serve**

Crushed cashews

Chopped cilantro

Lime wedges

1. Place the flour and salt in a large resealable plastic bag. Add the chicken thighs, seal the bag, and toss to coat.

2. Set the slow cooker to Saute and heat the coconut oil. Shake the excess flour from the chicken, add to the slow cooker, and brown on both sides, about 2 to 3 minutes per side.

3. Add the coconut milk, marinara sauce, onion, garlic, pineapple, lime, ginger, curry powder, turmeric, celery salt, and cumin. Stir to combine. Cover and cook on Low for 8 hours or High for 4 hours.

4. Allow to cool for 10 minutes and taste for seasoning before serving. Serve topped with cashews, cilantro, and a squeeze of lime.

**TIP** | If your slow cooker doesn't have a saute function, you can brown the chicken in a skillet on the stove and then transfer to the slow cooker. You can also omit the flour and skip step 1 altogether.

**VARIATION** | To make gluten-free, use a gluten-free flour.
For a thicker sauce, set to simmer and cook down until desired consistency is reached.

**NUTRITION PER SERVING (DOES NOT INCLUDE RICE OR NAAN)**

Calories **306**  •  Total Fat **24g**  •  Saturated Fat **12g**  •  Cholesterol **83mg**  •  Sodium **243mg**  •  Total Carbohydrate **9g**  •  Dietary Fiber **1g**  •  Sugars **3g**  •  Protein **16g**

# sausage + butternut soup

This hearty soup is easy enough for a weeknight dinner but impressive enough to serve for a dinner party. Cut the squash into large, equally sized pieces to prevent it from getting mushy.

Yield **6 servings** • Prep time **10 minutes** • Cook time **6 hours, 30 minutes**     FF

8 oz raw Italian chicken sausage

2 qt homemade or low-sodium chicken stock

1 (15oz) can diced tomatoes

4 cups diced butternut squash

1 tsp kosher salt

1 cup dry ditalini or elbow pasta

2 cups baby spinach

Parmesan cheese, to serve

1. Remove the casings from the sausages. Form the meat into small balls and place in the bottom of the slow cooker.

2. Add the chicken stock to the slow cooker, followed by the diced tomatoes, squash, and salt. Stir gently, cover, and set to cook for 6½ hours on High.

3. After 6 hours, stir in the pasta. Continue cooking for the remaining 30 minutes.

4. When the cook time is up, stir in the spinach. Serve hot, topped with Parmesan cheese.

5. Store leftovers in an airtight container in the refrigerator for up to 4 days or in the freezer for up to 3 months.

**NUTRITION PER SERVING**

Calories **430** • Total Fat **13g** • Saturated Fat **3g** • Cholesterol **87mg** • Sodium **689mg** •

Total Carbohydrate **37g** • Dietary Fiber **4g** • Sugars **5g** • Protein **36g**

# peanut chicken lettuce cups

Lettuce cups make for a healthy and effortless hand-held meal with minimal cleanup. With slow-cooked chicken, a tangy peanut sauce, and lots of fresh veggies piled on top, this low-carb, high-protein meal will definitely make your slow cooker hits list.

Yield **6 servings** • Prep time **10 minutes** • Cook time **6 hours**

1¾ lb boneless, skinless chicken thighs

2 tbsp reduced-sodium soy sauce (or gluten-free tamari)

1 tbsp rice vinegar

1 tbsp honey

2 cloves garlic, minced

¼ cup creamy peanut butter

½ head butter lettuce, leaves separated

1 cup grated carrots

½ jicama, cut into thin strips

½ cup chopped peanuts

Sriracha (optional), to serve

Lime wedges, to serve

**1.** Place chicken thighs in the slow cooker. In a small bowl, whisk together the soy sauce, vinegar, honey, and garlic.

**2.** Pour the sauce over the chicken and use tongs to turn the chicken, coating it completely with sauce. Cover and slow cook on High for 6 hours.

**3.** When the cook time is up, remove the lid and transfer ½ cup of the cooking liquid to a small bowl. (If you have less than ½ cup cooking liquid, add broth or water to reach ½ cup.) Add the peanut butter and whisk well to combine, adding additional liquid to thin out sauce, if desired.

**4.** Use tongs to break up chicken and then spoon into lettuce cups. Top chicken with peanut sauce, carrots, jicama, chopped peanuts, and Sriracha, if using. Serve with lime wedges.

**5.** Store leftovers in an airtight container in the refrigerator for up to 4 days.

**VARIATION** | Use cashew or almond butter instead of peanut butter.

**NUTRITION PER SERVING (ABOUT 3 LETTUCE CUPS WITH TOPPINGS)**

Calories **331** • Total Fat **17g** • Saturated Fat **3g** • Cholesterol **132mg** • Sodium **387mg** • Total Carbohydrate **11g** • Dietary Fiber **4g** • Sugars **5g** • Protein **35g**

# **chickpea** stew

This vegan stew has a secret ingredient. The canning liquid for the chickpeas, known as "aquafaba" thickens the soup and helps add to the depth of flavor. For a seasonal twist, add zucchini in the summer or potatoes in the winter.

Yield **8 servings** • Prep time **10 minutes** • Cook time **4 hours high/8 hours low**   GF  DF  V  FF

1 tbsp olive oil

1 small onion, diced

2 cloves garlic, chopped

1 tsp cumin seeds

1 tsp kosher salt

Pinch cayenne

2 (15oz) cans chickpeas

3 cups diced butternut squash

1 (15oz) can fire-roasted diced tomatoes

6 cups low-sodium vegetable broth

Parsley, chopped, to garnish

**1.** Set the slow cooker to Saute. Add the olive oil, onion, garlic, and cumin seeds, and cook for 5 minutes, until garlic is toasted and cumin seeds are fragrant. Turn off Saute mode.

**2.** Stir in the salt and cayenne. Rinse and drain 1 can of chickpeas and add to the slow cooker. Then add the second can of chickpeas along with the canning liquid. Add the squash, tomatoes, and vegetable broth. Stir to combine. Cover and cook for 4 hours on High or 8 hours on Low. Top with chopped parsley to garnish before serving.

**3.** Store leftovers in an airtight container in the refrigerator for up to 4 days or in the freezer for up to 3 months.

**VARIATION** | If your slow cooker doesn't have a sauté function, do step 1 on the stove top and add to the slow cooker.

**NUTRITION PER SERVING**

Calories **455** • Total Fat **8g** • Saturated Fat **0g** • Cholesterol **0mg** • Sodium **730mg** •

Total Carbohydrate **60g** • Dietary Fiber **20g** • Sugars **15g** • Protein **22g**

# **beef** stew

The slow cooker is the perfect one-pot cooking vessel for beef stew. You can add some baby potatoes to the last two hours of cooking, but I think this stew is better served over mashed potatoes, egg noodles, or polenta.

Yield **8 servings** • Prep time **10 minutes** • Cook time **4 hours high/8 hours low**

1 lb beef brisket, cubed

½ lb carrots, peeled and cut into large chunks

1 red onion, roughly chopped

1 tsp kosher salt

2 tsp dried thyme

½ tsp garlic powder

1 bay leaf

2 cups beef broth

2 tbsp tomato paste

3 tbsp chopped fresh parsley, to garnish

3 tbsp chopped fresh basil, to garnish

**1.** Place the beef, carrots, onion, salt, thyme, garlic powder, bay leaf, beef broth, tomato paste, and 1 cup water in a slow cooker. Cover and cook for 8 hours on Low or 4 hours on High.

**2.** When the cook time is up, remove the lid, stir, and taste for seasoning. Remove the bay leaf, and serve topped with chopped parsley and basil.

**3.** Leftovers can be stored in an airtight container in the refrigerator for up to 4 days or in the freezer for up to 3 months.

**VARIATION** | For a thicker stew, make a slurry of 1 tablespoon cornstarch and 2 tablespoons water and add for the last 30 minutes of cooking.

**NUTRITION PER SERVING**

Calories **355** • Total Fat **18g** • Saturated Fat **7g** • Cholesterol **102mg** • Sodium **548mg** •
Total Carbohydrate **4g** • Dietary Fiber **1g** • Sugars **2g** • Protein **40g**

# **chicken** cacciatore

I'm proud to say this recipe has been approved by family, friends, and kiddos alike. An easy, healthy, and tasty chicken dinner where the slow cooker does all the work! Serve with pasta, polenta, potatoes, or some crusty whole-grain bread, and you have yourself a nutritious, comforting meal.

Yield **6 servings**  •  Prep time **10 minutes**  •  Cook time **4 hours high/8 hours low**

½ cup all-purpose flour

½ tsp kosher salt

2 lb boneless, skinless chicken thighs

2 tsp olive oil

½ cup marinara sauce

½ cup chicken stock

½ red onion, sliced

1 clove garlic, thinly sliced

1 bell pepper, any color, sliced

Fresh basil, to garnish

Crushed red pepper flakes (optional), to serve

Parmesan cheese (optional), to serve

**1.** Place flour and salt in a large resealable bag. Add the chicken thighs, seal the bag, and shake to toss the chicken in flour.

**2.** Set the slow cooker to Saute and heat the olive oil. Shake the excess flour from the chicken, add to the slow cooker, and brown on both sides, about 2 to 3 minutes per side. Turn off sauté mode.

**3.** Add the marinara sauce, chicken stock, onion, garlic, and bell pepper. Cover and cook on Low for 8 hours or High for 4 hours.

**4.** Before serving, allow to cool for 10 minutes and taste for seasoning. Add additional salt if needed and top with fresh basil. Serve with red pepper flakes and Parmesan cheese, if desired.

**TIP** | If your slow cooker doesn't have a sauté function, you can brown the chicken in a skillet on the stove and then transfer to the slow cooker. You can also omit the flour and skip that step altogether.

**VARIATION** | To make dairy-free, leave out the Parmesan cheese or replace it with nutritional yeast (a flaky, yellow powder often used as a cheese substitute).

---

**NUTRITION PER SERVING (CHICKEN AND VEGETABLES ONLY)**

Calories **183**  •  Total Fat **6g**  •  Saturated Fat **1g**  •  Cholesterol **99mg**  •  Sodium **325mg**  •
Total Carbohydrate **8g**  •  Dietary Fiber **1g**  •  Sugars **2g**  •  Protein **23g**

# chicken noodle soup

You will be shocked how flavorful this chicken soup hack turns out after a few hours in the slow cooker. Prepare all the ingredients in a large releasable bag the night before for zero prep time the next morning.

Yield **6 servings**  •  Prep time **10 minutes**  •  Cook time **7 hours low**    **DF**  **FF**

1 cup chopped onion

1 cup chopped celery

1 cup chopped carrots

3 boneless, skinless chicken breasts

2 qt low-sodium or homemade chicken stock

1 tsp kosher salt

1 tsp dried thyme

1 tsp dried basil

1 cup wagon wheel or other small shaped pasta

3 cups shredded kale

**1.** Place the onion, celery, carrots, chicken, chicken stock, salt, thyme, and basil in the slow cooker. Cover and cook on Low for 6 to 7 hours

**2.** Remove the chicken breast, shred, and return to the slow cooker along with the pasta and kale. Cook on Low for 30 minutes more or until pasta is tender.

**3.** Store leftovers in airtight container in the refrigerator for up to 4 days or in the freezer for up to 3 months.

**TIP**  Taste your chicken stock ahead of time; if it isn't very flavorful, add ½ of a chicken bouillon cube to the recipe.

**NUTRITION PER SERVING**

Calories **356**  •  Total Fat **6g**  •  Saturated Fat **0.5g**  •  Cholesterol **130mg**  •  Sodium **435mg**  •
Total Carbohydrate **36g**  •  Dietary Fiber **3g**  •  Sugars **4g**  •  Protein **37g**

# sun-dried tomato risotto

You read that title correctly. Yes, you can make simply amazing risotto in your multicooker. No. Stirring. Required. This recipe turns a fancy and hard-to-prepare recipe into an effortless, one-pot weeknight meal.

Yield **4 servings**  •  Prep time **10 minutes**  •  Cook time **30 minutes**

1 tbsp olive oil

1 tbsp unsalted butter

1 small onion, finely chopped

¾ tsp kosher salt

¼ tsp freshly ground black pepper

1½ cups uncooked Arborio rice

3 tbsp dry white wine

3½ cups low-sodium or homemade chicken stock

¾ cup grated Parmesan cheese

½ cup sun-dried tomatoes, packed in oil, drained and chopped

½ cup chopped fresh parsley, to garnish

**1.** Set the multicooker to Saute (normal). Add the olive oil and butter. Once the butter has melted, add the onion, and sauté for 2 to 3 minutes until softened and translucent. Season with salt and pepper.

**2.** Add the rice and toss to coat in the oil. Turn off sauté mode and add wine to deglaze the pot.

**3.** Stir in the chicken stock. Cover and lock the lid, set the valve to the sealing position. Set to Pressure Cook (high) for 10 minutes.

**4.** When the cook time is up, allow the pressure to naturally release for 10 minutes, then manually release remaining pressure.

**5.** Remove the lid and stir in ½ cup cheese and ¼ cup sun-dried tomatoes.

**6.** Spoon into serving bowls and top individual servings with remaining cheese, sun-dried tomatoes, and parsley.

**TIP** | Set up a risotto bar and serve a variety of toppings such as olives, spinach, pine nuts, pesto, cooked chicken, caramelized onions, roasted squash, fresh herbs, chopped tomato, and steamed broccoli.

**NUTRITION PER SERVING**

Calories **522**  •  Total Fat **15g**  •  Saturated Fat **5g**  •  Cholesterol **21g**  •  Sodium **508mg**  •  Total Carbohydrate **78g**  •  Dietary Fiber **3g**  •  Sugars **5g**  •  Protein **19g**

# flank steak tacos
## with charred corn salsa

The best set-it-and-forget-it meal for taco lovers. Flank steak is one of the leanest cuts of beef, yet it's still incredibly flavorful and fall-apart tender when slow cooked. This is a great make-ahead recipe for busy weeknights any time of year.

Yield **6 servings** • Prep time **15 minutes** • Cook time **6–8 hours low**    GF  DF

Juice of ½ orange

1 clove garlic, finely chopped

1 tsp honey

1 tsp olive oil

1 tsp ground cumin

1 tsp smoked paprika

1 tsp kosher salt

½ tsp chili powder

½ tsp black pepper

2½ lb flank steak

1 yellow onion, sliced

12 (6-in) corn tortillas, to serve

**For the salsa**

2 ears corn, cooked

1 roasted red pepper, chopped

1 medium tomato, seeded and chopped

3 tbsp finely chopped red onion

Juice of 1 lime

2 tsp olive oil

½ cup chopped fresh cilantro

½ tsp kosher salt

3 dashes hot sauce

1. In a small bowl, combine the orange juice, garlic, honey, olive oil, cumin, smoked paprika, salt, chili powder, and black pepper.

2. Place the flank steak and onion in the slow cooker and pour the sauce over the top. Using tongs, turn the meat over a couple of times to ensure it is fully coated in sauce. Cover and set to slow cook on Low for 6 to 8 hours or until steak is tender and easily shredded.

3. To prepare the salsa, place the corn directly over an open flame on a gas burner on medium-high heat or under the broiler for 2 to 3 minutes per side or until charred as desired. Allow to cool slightly.

4. Once the corn is cool enough to handle, cut the kernels from the cob and place in a medium bowl. Add the roasted red pepper, tomato, red onion, lime juice, olive oil, cilantro, salt, and hot sauce. Stir and set aside.

5. When cook time is up, remove the slow cooker lid and drain away the cooking liquid, reserving about ⅓ cup. Shred the meat, adding back small amounts of the cooking liquid as desired.

6. Serve on warmed tortillas with charred corn salsa. Optional toppings include Greek yogurt, avocado, radish, and lime juice.

**TIP** | If fresh corn is unavailable, you can substitute frozen corn. Defrost 1 cup and char in a dry skillet over high heat.

---

**NUTRITION PER SERVING (2 TACOS WITH SALSA)**

Calories **485** • Total Fat **18g** • Saturated Fat **6g** • Cholesterol **123mg** • Sodium **323mg** •
Total Carbohydrate **37g** • Dietary Fiber **5g** • Sugars **6g** • Protein **45g**

# salsa verde **chicken**

This two-ingredient recipe (plus a couple of spices) is a weeknight-meal game changer for boring chicken breast. Serve with brown rice or layer between corn tortillas with some gooey melted cheese. Make a big batch for weekly meal prep for dinners and lunches to get you through a busy week.

Yield **4 servings**  •  Prep time **5 minutes**  •  Cook time **30 minutes**

1lb boneless, skinless chicken breast

1 tsp smoked paprika

½ tsp kosher salt

1 cup salsa verde

1. Place the chicken, paprika, salt, and salsa in the inner pot.

2. Cover and lock the lid, set the valve to the sealing position, and set to Pressure Cook (high) for 20 minutes. When the cook time is complete, allow the pressure to naturally release.

3. Remove the lid, transfer the chicken to a plate and shred. Serve with additional salsa verde if desired.

---

**NUTRITION PER SERVING**

Calories **272**  •  Total Fat **5g**  •  Saturated Fat **0g**  •  Cholesterol **143mg**  •  Sodium **430mg**  •  Total Carbohydrate **3g**  •  Dietary Fiber **0g**  •  Sugars **1g**  •  Protein **30g**

# crazy good **lentil soup**

Confession time: I am not a fan of lentil soup. Since there is no denying the superfood qualities of this little legume, I set out to make this soup—a lentil soup so yummy, even I crave it! Did I mention it is bursting with flavor, plus chockful of fiber and protein?

Yield **6 servings** • Prep time **10 minutes** • Cook time **45 minutes**    GF  DF  FF

2 tsp olive oil

1 garlic clove, minced

1 small onion, chopped

2 cups diced butternut squash

1 small sweet potato, peeled and diced

2 cups chopped carrots

1 cup chopped celery

1½ cups green lentils, rinsed and drained

1 tsp kosher salt

1 tsp ground turmeric

1 tsp dried thyme

½ tsp ground cumin

6 cups low-sodium or homemade chicken or vegetable stock

4 cups baby kale or spinach

**1.** To the inner pot, add the olive oil, garlic, onion, squash, sweet potato, carrots, celery, lentils, salt, turmeric, thyme, cumin, chicken stock, and 1 cup water. Stir well.

**2.** Cover and lock the lid, set the valve to the sealing position, and select the Soup/Stew mode for 30 minutes.

**3.** When the cook time is complete, quick release the pressure. Remove the lid and stir in the baby kale. Taste for seasoning (see tip) and serve.

**4.** Store leftovers in airtight container in the refrigerator for up to 4 days or in the freezer for up to 3 months.

**TIP** | If you'd like to cut the earthy flavor of the lentils, stir in 2 to 3 teaspoons of red wine or sherry vinegar just before serving.

**NUTRITION PER SERVING**

Calories **256** • Total Fat **2g** • Saturated Fat **0g** • Cholesterol **0mg** • Sodium **508mg** •

Total Carbohydrate **43g** • Dietary Fiber **18g** • Sugars **5g** • Protein **16g**

# spicy shrimp ramen

Ramen has come a long way from the college dorm room. You can make a flavorful and nutrient-rich broth in minutes using a multicooker. This low-calorie meal is filled with lean protein, probiotics, and fresh vegetables. It's just as good for your soul as it is for your body—get slurping.

Yield **4 servings** • Prep time **10 minutes** • Cook time **40 minutes**    DF  FF

1-in piece fresh ginger, peeled

2 pieces kombu

2 cloves garlic, peeled

1 tbsp white miso paste

3 tbsp reduced-sodium soy sauce

2 tsp Sriracha, plus more for serving

10 oz uncooked ramen noodles (such as China Bowl brand)

8 oz large shrimp, peeled and deveined

1 cup grated carrots

3 cups baby spinach

**1.** Add 8 cups water to the inner pot, followed by the ginger, kombu, and garlic. Cover and lock the lid, and set the valve to the sealing position. Set to Pressure Cook (high) for 10 minutes.

**2.** When the cook time is up, quick release the pressure and remove the lid. Using a slotted spoon or small sieve, remove the kombu and any other remnants of ginger and garlic. Whisk in the miso, soy sauce, and Sriracha.

**3.** Set to Saute (high) and bring the broth to a simmer. Once simmering, add the noodles and shrimp and cook for 3 minutes or until noodles are tender.

**4.** Turn off the heat. Using tongs, divide the noodles and shrimp evenly among 4 serving bowls. Add equal portions of carrots and spinach to each bowl and ladle the broth over top. Serve with additional Sriracha if desired.

**5.** The broth freezes beautifully. Strain and store in a freezer-safe container for up to 3 months. To reheat, boil fresh noodles in water and serve with vegetables and reheated broth.

**TIP** | This recipe is designed to be made in one pot, if you want to make ahead, keep the noodles and broth separate until ready to serve.

**VARIATION** | Mushrooms and kale also work well in this dish.

**NUTRITION PER SERVING**

Calories **355** • Total Fat **3g** • Saturated Fat **0g** • Cholesterol **107mg** • Sodium **624mg** •

Total Carbohydrate **60g** • Dietary Fiber **8g** • Sugars **5g** • Protein **22g**

# pulled **pork**

With a multicooker, delicious and endlessly versatile pulled pork becomes a quick, weeknight meal. Serve it with lettuce wraps, over rice, in a burrito, or on a bun—or just enjoy on its own. Using a 6-quart pot or larger, this recipe can easily be doubled to feed a crowd.

Yield **6**  •  Prep time **5 minutes**  •  Cook time **30 minutes**

2 (1lb) pork tenderloins, each cut into 3 pieces

1 red onion, sliced

½ cup barbecue sauce (Trader Joe's brand recommended)

1 tsp kosher salt

½ tsp freshly ground black pepper

½ ground fennel seed

**1.** Place the pork in the inner pot along with the onion, barbecue sauce, salt, pepper, and fennel. Mix gently to coat the pork in the spices.

**2.** Fasten the lid, set the valve to the sealing position, and set to Pressure Cook (high) for 25 minutes. When the cook time is up, quick release the pressure.

**3.** Remove 1 cup of the cooking liquid and set aside. Shred the pork. Add the reserved cooking liquid as needed along with more barbecue sauce, if desired. Serve pulled pork on sandwich rolls, rice bowls, or in salads or burritos.

**NUTRITION PER SERVING**

Calories **201**  •  Total Fat **3g**  •  Saturated Fat **1g**  •  Cholesterol **73mg**  •  Sodium **540mg**  •  Total Carbohydrate **10g**  •  Dietary Fiber **0g**  •  Sugars **4g**  •  Protein **31g**

# simple **rice + beans**

Rice and beans are a staple in so many cultures because they contain a perfect balance of protein-building amino acids. The multicooker makes it easy to enjoy this traditional pairing, no presoaking required. Excellent on their own, you can also serve rice and beans with grilled meat, in a salad, or wrapped in a burrito.

Yield **4 servings** • Prep time **5 minutes** • Cook time **35 minutes**

1 cup uncooked black beans, drained and rinsed

1 bay leaf

1 green bell pepper, diced

1 cup uncooked brown rice, rinsed

¼ tsp salt

Fresh cilantro, chopped, to serve

**1.** Place the beans, bay leaf, green pepper, and 2½ cups water in the inner pot. Place a metal trivet over the beans.

**2.** In a small, oven-safe dish, combine the brown rice with 1 cup water and salt. Place the dish on the trivet.

**3.** Cover and lock the lid, set the valve to the sealing position, and set to Pressure Cook (high) for 25 minutes.

**4.** When the cook time is complete, allow the pressure to naturally release for 15 minutes, then quick release any remaining pressure.

**5.** Remove the lid, remove the rice and fluff with a fork. Stir the beans well and season with salt and pepper to taste.

**6.** To serve, ladle the beans over the cooked rice. Top with fresh cilantro.

**VARIATION** | Make a rice and bean salad by mixing cooked rice and beans with chopped tomato, diced mango, chopped scallions, and a squeeze of fresh lime juice.

**NUTRITION PER SERVING**

Calories **346** • Total Fat **2g** • Saturated Fat **0.5g** • Cholesterol **0mg** • Sodium **154mg** •
Total Carbohydrate **68g** • Dietary Fiber **10g** • Sugars **3g** • Protein **15g**

# **lobster** boil

Lobster becomes easy enough for a weeknight meal with your multicooker. This delicate seafood can go from freezer to table in 15 minutes—no thawing required. Serve with biscuits and a green salad for a complete meal.

Yield **2 servings**  •  Prep time **5 minutes**  •  Cook time **15 minutes**         GF  DF  30

2 frozen lobster tails

2 ears of corn, cut in half

Butter, melted, to serve

Lemon wedges, to serve

**1.** Place a trivet in the bottom of the inner pot along with 1 cup water.

**2.** Using a sturdy knife or poultry shears, cut a slit in the back of the shell of each lobster. Place the tails shell-side up on the trivet. Place the pieces of corn on the trivet along with the lobster.

**3.** Cover and lock the lid, set the valve to the sealing position, and set to Pressure Cook (high) for 4 minutes. (If using lobster that is not frozen, reduce the cook time to 2 minutes.)

**4.** When the cook time is complete, quick release the pressure. Using tongs, remove the lobster tails and corn. Cut the lobster tails in half lengthwise.

**5.** Serve with melted butter and lemon wedges. Leftover lobster meat can be removed from the shells and stored in an airtight container in the refrigerator for up to 2 days.

---

**NUTRITION PER SERVING (DOES NOT INCLUDE BUTTER)**

Calories **300**  •  Total Fat **3g**  •  Saturated Fat **0.5g**  •  Cholesterol **372mg**  •  Sodium **201mg**  •
Total Carbohydrate **14g**  •  Dietary Fiber **2g**  •  Sugars **2g**  •  Protein **25g**

# maple-dijon salmon
## with sweet potatoes

Trying to eat more salmon? It helps if it can be ready in minutes! Salmon is a great source of omega-3 fats, which help fight inflammation and benefit your skin, memory, vision, immunity, and cardiovascular health.

Yield **2 servings** • Prep time **3 minutes** • Cook time **5 minutes**    **GF** **DF** **30**

2 medium sweet potatoes, peeled and diced

½ tsp kosher salt

1 tsp olive oil, plus more to serve

2 (5oz) pieces skinless frozen salmon

1 tsp Dijon mustard

1 tsp maple syrup

2 slices lemon

8 oz baby arugula

Freshly squeezed lemon juice, to serve

**1.** Place the sweet potato in the bottom of the inner pot. Add ½ cup water, salt and olive oil and mix gently.

**2.** Spray a wire rack with cooking spray and place inside the pot on top of the sweet potatoes. Place the salmon on the rack.

**3.** In a small bowl, mix the mustard and maple syrup. Brush the mustard mixture on the salmon and top each piece with a lemon slice.

**4.** Cover and lock the lid. Place the vent in the sealing position. Set to Pressure Cook (high) for 5 minutes. When the cook time is up, quick release the pressure and remove the lid.

**5.** Remove the salmon and the rack and mash the sweet potatoes with a fork.

**6.** To serve, arrange a bed of arugula on a plate, drizzle with additional olive oil, a squeeze of fresh lemon juice, and a sprinkle of sea salt. Top with mashed sweet potato and salmon.

**TIP** | If you have fresh salmon on hand, cut down the cook time by 2 minutes and cut the sweet potatoes a little bit smaller to ensure even and complete cooking.

**NUTRITION PER SERVING**

Calories **349** • Total Fat **11g** • Saturated Fat **2g** • Cholesterol **64g** • Sodium **447mg** •
Total Carbohydrate **29g** • Dietary Fiber **4g** • Sugars **8g** • Protein **33g**

# shrimp + grits

Tender shrimp in a tangy sauce poured over a creamy and cheesy pile of grits. This southern comfort dish is usually drenched in butter, cream, and tons of cheese, but it can be made with a fraction of the calories with just a few adjustments. A small amount of full-flavored cheese goes a long way.

Yield **4 servings** • Prep time **8 minutes** • Cook time **10 minutes**

2 tbsp unsalted butter, divided

1 tbsp olive oil

12 oz raw shrimp, peeled and deveined

1 clove garlic, minced

½ tsp dried thyme

½ cup chopped roasted red pepper

½ tsp smoked paprika

½ tsp kosher salt

2 tsp fresh thyme

½ tsp crushed red pepper flakes

Juice and zest of ½ lemon

½ cup grits

½ cup grated sharp cheddar cheese

2 tbsp chopped scallions, to garnish

**1.** Set the pot to Saute (normal) and add 1 tablespoon butter and olive oil. Add the shrimp and garlic and sauté for 2 minutes. Add the thyme and roasted red pepper and season with smoked paprika, salt, thyme, red pepper flakes, and lemon juice. Continue to sauté for 3 to 5 minutes until shrimp is opaque.

**2.** Turn off the heat. Transfer the shrimp and sauce to a bowl, cover with aluminum foil, and set aside.

**3.** Without cleaning out the inner pot, add the remaining 1 tablespoon butter and grits. Stir in 2 cups water. Cover and lock the lid. Place the vent in the sealing position and set to Pressure Cook (high) for 10 minutes. Allow the pressure to naturally release for 10 minutes before releasing the remaining pressure manually.

**4.** Remove the lid and stir in cheese and lemon zest and continue to stir until cheese is melted and grits are creamy. Scoop the grits onto a platter and top with shrimp and scallions. Serve immediately.

---

**NUTRITION PER SERVING**

Calories **275** • Total Fat **13g** • Saturated Fat **6g** • Cholesterol **161g** • Sodium **311mg** •

Total Carbohydrate **19g** • Dietary Fiber **2g** • Sugars **3g** • Protein **21g**

# kale + white bean soup

Multicookers were made for soups like this. A flavorful one-pot mixture of wholesome vegetables, beans, and lean protein in a savory broth seasoned with fennel and rosemary. Complete the meal with crusty, whole-grain bread.

Yield **6 servings** • Prep time **10 minutes** • Cook time **40 minutes**     GF  FF

1 tbsp olive oil

12 oz raw chicken sausage, casings removed

½ tsp ground fennel seed

½ cup chopped onion

3 garlic cloves, chopped

1 bunch kale, stems removed and chopped

1 tbsp chopped fresh rosemary

2 tsp balsamic vinegar

1 tsp kosher salt

Freshly ground black pepper

1 qt low-sodium or homemade chicken stock

1 (15oz) can cannellini beans, rinsed and drained

½ cup grated Parmesan cheese

Crusty whole-grain bread (optional), to serve

**1.** Set the pot to Saute (normal) and add the olive oil. Once oil is heated, add the chicken sausage and fennel and sauté until the chicken begins to brown. Add the onion, garlic, and kale, stir, and cook for 1 to 2 minutes. Add the rosemary, vinegar, salt, and pepper. Cook for 5 to 6 minutes more.

**2.** Turn off the heat and stir in the chicken stock. Cover and lock the lid, set the valve to the sealing position, and set to Pressure Cook (high) for 7 minutes.

**3.** Quick release the pressure and carefully remove the lid. Stir in the beans and cover. Let sit with the heat off for 5 minutes. Ladle into bowls and serve topped with Parmesan cheese and a side of crusty bread, if desired.

**4.** Once cooled, transfer to an airtight container and store in the refrigerator for up to 4 days or the freezer for up to 3 months.

**TIP** | If freezing, omit the Parmesan cheese until you reheat.

**VARIATION** | For a vegetarian version, skip the chicken and double up on the beans, swap vegetable broth in for the chicken broth. You can also add diced carrots or canned diced tomatoes.

---

**NUTRITION PER SERVING (DOES NOT INCLUDE BREAD)**

Calories **312** • Total Fat **13g** • Saturated Fat **5g** • Cholesterol **98g** • Sodium **838mg** •

Total Carbohydrate **19g** • Dietary Fiber **6g** • Sugars **3g** • Protein **24g**

# sausage-stuffed mini peppers (freezer mezal)

This hearty freezer meal can be prepared in bulk on a meal-prep day and then pulled out and cooked as needed. Serve these savory stuffed peppers with a side of pasta or quinoa or a green salad for a low-carb dinner.

Yield **4 servings**  •  Prep time **15 minutes** •  Cook time **3 hours high/6 hours low**

1 (16oz) bag mini peppers

1 lb raw chicken sausage, casings removed

2 cups marinara sauce

Fresh basil, chopped, to garnish

**1.** Cut the tops off the mini peppers and use a small spoon or paring knife to remove any seeds.

**2.** Fill each pepper with chicken sausage (see tip) and transfer to a gallon-size resealable bag in an even layer.

**3.** Once all the peppers have been filled, place the bag on a sheet pan and place in the freezer to set. (The peppers can remain frozen for up to 3 months before using.) Allow the peppers to defrost in the refrigerator overnight before cooking.

**4.** To cook, pour the marinara sauce in the bottom of a slow cooker and arrange the defrosted peppers on top. Cook on Low for 6 hours or High for 3 hours. Serve garnished with fresh basil.

**TIP** | To help fill the peppers, place the raw chicken sausage in a resealable plastic bag. Cut the corner of the bag with chicken shears and pipe the sausage into the peppers.

**VARIATION** | For a cheesy topping, sprinkle with cheese for the last 15 minutes of cooking.

---

**NUTRITION PER SERVING**

Calories **319**  •  Total Fat **7g**  •  Saturated Fat **2g**  •  Cholesterol **131mg**  •  Sodium **723mg**  •
Total Carbohydrate **20g**  •  Dietary Fiber **5.5g**  •  Sugars **10g**  •  Protein **43g**

# sweet potato coconut stew (freezer meal)

This cozy, creamy vegan stew will save the day on one of those nights when you've totally spaced on what to make for dinner. Go from freezer to slow cooker in the morning, and you'll have a hearty stew waiting for dinner.

Yield **6 servings**  •  Prep time **15 minutes**  •  Cook time **4 hours high/6 hours low**     GF   DF   V   FF

1 lb sweet potatoes, peeled and diced

½ (28oz) can crushed tomatoes

1 (15oz) can coconut milk

1 (15oz) can black beans, drained and rinsed

1 jalapeño, thinly sliced

1 small red onion, diced

3 cloves garlic, finely chopped

½ tsp turmeric

1 tsp curry powder

½ tsp ground cumin

1 tsp kosher salt

1 cup chopped cashews

Cooked rice (optional), to serve

Fresh cilantro, chopped, to garnish

**1.** In a large resealable plastic bag, combine the sweet potato, crushed tomatoes, coconut milk, black beans, jalapeno, onion, garlic, turmeric, curry powder, cumin, and salt.

**2.** Seal the bag and lay flat to freeze.

**3.** When ready to cook, add the frozen mixture to a slow cooker and cook on High for 4 hours or Low for 6 hours

**4.** When the cook time is up, remove the lid and stir. Serve over cooked rice, if desired, and top with fresh cilantro.

**TIP** | To save time, use 1 pound frozen sweet potato chunks in place of fresh sweet potatoes.

---

**NUTRITION PER SERVING (DOES NOT INCLUDE RICE)**

Calories **423**  •  Total Fat **25g**  •  Saturated Fat **16g**  •  Cholesterol **0mg**  •  Sodium **544mg**  •

Total Carbohydrate **43g**  •  Dietary Fiber **11g**  •  Sugars **8g**  •  Protein **11g**

# index

## H–I–J

## K

## L

## M

## N–O–P

## Q–R